HOLY SPIRIT COME

Releasing Your Spiritual Gifts

New Expanded Edition—Bible Study Guide

CONNIE ENGEL

constant byword

HOLY SPIRIT COME

Releasing Your Spiritual Gifts

New Expanded Edition—Bible Study Guide
(The Art of Charismatic Christian Living: Book One)

Written by Connie Engel

Kindly direct all inquiries about this book to:
constantbyword@aol.com

Excepting brief excerpts for review purposes, no part of this book or its cover image can be used without written permission from the author.

Except as otherwise noted, all Scripture quotations are taken from the New American Standard Bible ® Copyright © 1960, 1962, 1963, 1968, 1971, 1972, 1973, 1975, 1977, 1995 by The Lockman Foundation used by permission. (www.Lockman.org)

Most names in anecdotes in this book have been changed to protect the privacy of those involved.

Cover image: "Blue Night," oil on canvas,
by Connie Engel.

ISBN: 9781729418956

Copyright © 2018, Connie Engel,
all rights reserved.

Published in the United States of America
Third Edition 2018

HOLY SPIRIT COME

Releasing Your Spiritual Gifts

"The longer I am in ministry and the more pressing needs I see around the world, the more I cry, 'Holy Spirit Come.' Connie Engel has written a helpful, thoughtful, and Scripture-packed book that will add fuel to the fire of your spiritual passion. Read it with your Bible open as it will provoke your thinking."

—Gary Wilkerson
President, *World Challenge*

"While working as an actress in the midst of Hollywood, I began a new life as a Christian and had the great blessing of being introduced to Connie Engel. An author and spiritual mentor. Because her own walk is Spirit-led, she is able to lead others, like me, effortlessly into a deeper intimacy with the Holy Spirit and a greater understanding of spiritual gifts. This book has blessed me tremendously. It is a must read!"

—Alley Mills
Actress, *The Wonder Years, The Bold and the Beautiful*

This book is dedicated to every believer who truly longs for an intimate and personal relationship with the amazing Holy Spirit. Who earnestly desires to be gifted by Him with the supernatural Spiritual and Service gifts He so generously offers to all. May each reader receive their gifts and be prepared to use them as the Spirit leads for the days ahead to bless, edify, and strengthen the Body of Christ.

CONTENTS

SECTION ONE

The Holy Spirit and His Supernatural Spiritual Gifts

Chapters 1—11

Preface	13
1 Who is the Holy Spirit?	17
2 The Holy Spirit's Purpose	35
3 How to Receive the Holy Spirit	49
4 Words of Wisdom and Knowledge	67

5
The Gift of Faith   85

6
Gifts of Healing   99

7
The Effecting of Miracles   113

8
The Gift of Prophecy   131

9
Discerning of Spirits   147

10
Tongues—the Heavenly Language   157

11
Ordinary People   169

SECTION TWO

Service Gifts
of the Holy Spirit

Chapters 12—28

12 Many Ways to Serve	187
13 The Gift of Serving	199
14 The Gift of Leadership	209
15 The Gift of Exhortation	223
16 The Gift of Giving	235
17 The Gift of Mercy	247

18
The Gift of Teaching   257

19
The Gift of Ministering   267

20
The Gift of Apostleship   275

21
The Gift of Helps   285

22
The Gift of Administration   293

23
The Gift of Evangelism   301

24
The Gift of a Pastor   309

25
Other Gifts   317

26
How to Receive Your Gifts   329

27
How to Use Your Gifts   339

28 Holy Spirit Come	347
Afterword	351
About the Author	355
Books by Connie Engel	357

PREFACE

My Dear Friend,

Joy fills my heart in having this opportunity to share the most amazing part of my life with you. Living with the Holy Spirit. The excitement of being used by Him for His glory. This admiration of mine doesn't take away from the other two Members of the Trinity, but instead, brings them all together as One. I love each part of God equally. But to share about this one very special part of God, is a true blessing. My prayer is that I may do it in truth with the help of the Helper, Himself, with the Word of God, faith stories of others, and my own unique experiences.

The Holy Spirit comes to live in normal, ordinary people like you and me. He waits for us to call upon Him and ask Him into our lives, our families, and ministries—then corrects, perfects, and affects all things as much as we will allow Him. And now more than ever before, in this world of growing darkness, we need His power and gifting.

My soul bursts with love for the Father, Son, and Holy Spirit. Each has His own purpose and personality that blends into a perfect God. As we learn by studying His Word, His ways, and by yielding to Him, we will be used to do wondrous things for His kingdom, while giving Him all the glory. That only He deserves.

Excitement rises up within me as I begin to write this book. I faithfully pray that the words herein will permeate from the pages and embed themselves into the depth of your heart.

THE FOCUS: To depict the supernatural power of our God through His Spirit, and His supernatural gifts for you. To describe the gifts in full, in order to present to you a clear picture of God's purposes in your personal life and ministry.

There are two sections in this book. The first one will reflect on and project the multitude of facets and blessings that are hidden within the supernatural spiritual gifts of the Holy Spirit. The second one will describe and explore the Holy Spirit-led service gifts. Each gift in every chapter of this book is explained in depth accompanied with Scriptures. My own, and others' personal experiences with the gifts, will be threaded throughout to implement a personal touch that you can relate to. There will be questions at the end of each chapter that will challenge you to submit to and desire more of God's Spirit.

How much will you yield to receive what God has for you? As you look deeply within your own heart, you will grow and mature in the Holy Spirit. As you address the questions herein, you'll identify and better understand the gifts. I pray that they will help to open your spiritual eyes to see God's will in your life and His purposes for you in His glory.

While you read ahead, keep in mind to pray at the beginning of each chapter for the Holy Spirit to speak to you and enable you to apprehend the gifts He's bestowed upon you. And to learn how to ignite them and apply them.

Thank you for letting me share my heart with you. To help bring you into a complete and clear understanding of the Holy Spirit and what He desires to do in and through you.

My love in Christ,
Connie

SECTION ONE

THE HOLY SPIRIT AND HIS SUPERNATURAL GIFTS

"Now there are varieties of gifts, but the same Spirit. And there are varieties of ministries, and the same Lord. There are varieties of effects, but the same God who works all things in all persons. But to each one is given the manifestation of the Spirit for the common good. For to one is given the word of wisdom through the Spirit, and to another the word of knowledge according to the same Spirit; to another faith by the same Spirit, and to another gifts of healing by the one Spirit, and to another the effecting of miracles, and to another prophecy, and to another the distinguishing of spirits, to another various kinds of tongues, and to another the interpretation of tongues. But one and the same Spirit works all these things, distributing to each one individually just as He wills."

1 Corinthians 12:4–11

1

Who is the Holy Spirit?

"But the Helper, the Holy Spirit, whom the Father will send in My name, He will teach you all things, and bring to your remembrance all that I said to you."

John 14:26

The Holy Spirit is my guide in everything I do. In all of my imaginings, never could I had thought up the magnitude of supernatural occurrences that have taken place in my life, and in the life of others. I've witnessed blessings by the movement of the Holy Spirit and the gifts He gives to us. I've been amazed as I've seen God's hand perform miracles as He led me to minister in the power of the Holy Spirit.

Ever since I was born again, He has used me to bring forth many miracles, healings, and awesome works in Jesus' powerful name. From day to day, His glorious manifestations would unfold before my eyes, and the eyes of those around me. At each turn of events, I'd be greatly moved by His spontaneity and willingness to use an imperfect person such as myself.

I would love to share a portion of the miraculous things I've witnessed Him do, in order to project a picture of His power and greatness. And He only is worthy. I give all of the glory to Him. Below are several, concise descriptions of the Holy Spirit's supernatural accomplishments:

•

As the Lord led me, I prayed for a young mother's brain tumor to dissolve the day before she had surgery. The next morning, during that operation, the surgeon found nothing but dried up blood where the tumor had been. Our loving God also kept the baby in her womb safe from the possible deformities that surgery might cause.

•

A friend's husband died, and the Lord asked me to call him back in Jesus' name. I obeyed God and He brought him back in order for him to ask forgiveness from family members, who were at his bedside. Later that day, he died again. And departed for heaven.

•

The Lord instructed me to pray that no weapon formed against my friend, Danny, would prosper. After two weeks of prayer, I heard on the news of a gunman inside the building where he worked. Three of our other friends were tragically killed. Danny miraculously escaped, while also helping other employees out of the store to safety.

WHO IS THE HOLY SPIRIT?

On an Easter Sunday years ago, God multiplied the food for the twenty unexpected people that showed up for dinner. Every guest witnessed the miracle, and had plenty of food to eat. And afterward were awestruck by the amount of food that remained.

•

Not long after my new life in Christ, God had promised me two sons, very close together in age. One with darker skin, brown hair, and brown eyes. The other with lighter skin, blond hair, and blue eyes. A short time later, after I had been diagnosed with endometriosis, my doctor told me that I'd become completely sterile and couldn't have children. I knew God would heal me because He is a God who doesn't lie. He had made me a promise, and I knew He wouldn't break it. Our faithful God did heal me. I had my two boys. They both looked exactly the way He had described them to me.

•

These are some of my stories. It's possible that you've heard similar stories that have been a great source of encouragement to you. Or perhaps you've heard of other stories that have spread around this world about the Holy Spirit that seem off. Not true. In many cases, they've caused people to be afraid of Him, and run from Him. Maybe they've even led some to mock Him. Someone they don't know or understand.

I've been asked many questions about my walk with God. Especially ones about the Holy Spirit and the gifts He has so generously given to me. A person once asked me how I could be alright with a spirit living within me, expounding on the very weirdness of it. I explained that it isn't any old spirit, and not a dark one as well, but the Spirit of almighty God, who made the universe and everything within it. Including mankind.

The Holy Spirit is a gentleman. He only resides in us if we invite Him to. If God blew breath into us to come alive, why wouldn't we want that very breath of life to blossom within us? To change our hearts and the way we view things? We need to only ask with a sincere heart. And when we do, He appears at the door of our hearts, happily, to dwell within us. He desires to commune with us and work with us for the sake of God and His kingdom. He gives us all that we need to sojourn with God during our stays here on earth. With Him, we will have no lack.

As the great evangelist, Billy Graham once said: "The church today has all of the tools for conquest—money, edifices, organizations, education, and methods. But we lack the God-given spark to ignite these things into a spiritual fire that could sweep the world and help bring peace to our desperate world. That spark is the personal infilling of the Holy Spirit in the life of every believer, without which the church has no spiritual power."

As we continue on our exploration of the amazing Holy Spirit, His gifts and miraculous ways, let's form a solid foundation to build our faith upon. Cementing one revelation at a time to produce a strong, healthy, and everlasting relationship with Him. To learn more about the Holy Spirit will give us greater understanding of how to draw wisdom from Him and to be led by His anointing. It will enable us to develop spiritual ears to hear His divine direction through an intimate communication. One crisply clear, like we've never experienced.

When we dig deeper into the unspeakable greatness of His ways and miraculous power, a closeness will develop. A unique bonding into one with Him will occur.

A life of glory is awaiting those of us who have not yet tasted that the Lord is good. Truly delicious, as a matter of fact. Unlike anything we've ever touched or seen. The invisible glory that comes to dwell within us and brings forth a fountain of living water that springs up from our very cores to graciously perform and witness the miraculous.

There are a multitude of questions asked about the Holy Spirit. You may have asked a few of these yourself. I will address several of them as we journey along through this book. We'll start with this one:

Who is the Holy Spirit?

This question has been asked throughout time, since God created man. People have often wondered if the Holy Spirit is the spirit of the living God. If He is invisible, or whether He has a form. They've questioned the purposes and functions of Him, and how they should connect with Him. The mystery of how the Holy Spirit can live within us has puzzled many. The inquiries are endless. To find out the answers, and to learn as much as we can, I'd like to explore every aspect of the Holy Spirit with you.

Let's start with a definition of this glorious part of God:

The word for spirit in the Greek is *pneuma;* "the wind" (akin "to breathe, blow, breath in"); also "the spirit" which like the wind, is powerful and immaterial, but invisible.

The Holy Spirit is the third Person of the Trinity, who lives inside of believers. He is our Helper, who directs us in all ways. He graciously gives us power in the name of Jesus, who told us that

He would come. The Holy Spirit helps us grow in our knowledge of God and His holiness. He is our guide and our teacher. He is a revealer of truth. A great, priceless treasure He is. One to trust and wholly embrace. Never to shun or exclude. The benefits of His presence are endless. He waits for us to yield, as our hearts hunger to be used by Him.

Why is the Holy Spirit such a mystery?

Throughout history there has been a mystery within the truths of Christianity. The quest: "Who and what is the Holy Spirit?" Many people are asking the same question today. Even Christians.

This is a subject that has delighted some, but with others—stirred great suspense and division within the Body at large. In ancient Israel, the Holy Spirit dwelt *among* men. And since the Day of Pentecost, the Holy Spirit dwells *within* men. This might sound odd to those who have not yet had the enormous blessing of knowing Him personally.

Let's look at a little history. Do you know when the Holy Spirit was first mentioned? He actually showed up in the Old Testament. Below, we see that the Psalmist, David, cries out to God to not take His Holy Spirit from him:

"Do not cast me away from Your presence and do not take Your Holy Spirit from me."

Psalm 51:11

David cried out this heartfelt request to God as part of his repentance prayer. He'd be truly devastated to live without the presence of the Holy Spirit in his life. David acknowledged his transgression and confessed that his sin remained continually before him. As ours do as well. The same temptations exist today as they did from the beginning of creation.

In David's case, he knew the necessity of repentance in getting back to the oneness he had with His Lord. He also realized that He had sinned directly against God.

I am grateful that we have a loving Lord who forgives. I don't know about you, but I have sinned much in my life. Sin separates us from God's presence. And when that void hovers over us, the dank darkness of evil is palpable.

David's deep desire for God to restore and transform his heart became first among any other. He acknowledged it to be the only source of renewal, and pleaded with God to create a clean, pure heart within him. He did so with the understanding that his heart had to be in that condition once again before he could experience God's presence.

David had been empowered by the Holy Spirit:

"Then Samuel took the horn of oil and anointed him in the midst of his brothers; and the Spirit of the Lord came mightily upon David from that day forward."

1 Samuel 16:13

The Messiah would also be empowered by the Spirit:

"Behold, My Servant [Jesus] whom I uphold; My chosen one in whom My soul delights. I have put My Spirit upon Him; He will bring forth justice to the nations."

Isaiah 42:1

The people who first read these old Hebrew Scriptures might have viewed the sayings about God's Spirit as a way of speaking of God's marvelous character and His wonders. In the New

Testament, we are charged with going forth in the name of the Holy Spirit, as the third Person of the Trinity—to baptize others and make them disciples of Christ:

> *"Go therefore and make disciples of all the nations, baptizing them in the name of the Father, and the Son, and the Holy Spirit."*
> Matthew 28:19

These words are those of the Messiah, Jesus. Clearly, the Holy Spirit is part of the Trinity of God. The Father, the Son, and the Holy Spirit make up this Trio. Three in One. Foretold of in the book of Isaiah:

> *"Come near to Me, listen to this: From the first I have not spoken in secret, from the time it took place, I was there. And now the Lord GOD has sent Me, and His Spirit."*
> Isaiah 48:16

The Holy Spirit had an active part in orchestrating the birth of God's own Son. Mary was found with child by His works. God ordained Joseph and Mary to be the legal, earthly parents of Jesus, not diminishing the miraculous conception:

> *"Now the birth of Jesus Christ was as follows: when His mother Mary had been betrothed to Joseph, before they came together she was found to be with child by the Holy Spirit."*
> Matthew 1:18

All part of God's perfect plan to bring forth His Son into this world to save us. Jesus not only came for that reason, but also to baptize us with the Holy Spirit, before He ascended into heaven, as John the Baptist had proclaimed to so many:

"As for me, I baptize you with water for repentance, but He who is coming after me is mightier than I, and I am not fit to remove His sandals; He will baptize you with the Holy Spirit and fire."
Matthew 3:11

John knew that there would be a great presentation and clear evidence of the Holy Spirit in the lives of believers. Promises of the divine Holy Spirit to come are in the following Scriptures:

"Until the Spirit is poured out upon us from on high, and the wilderness becomes a fertile field, and the fertile field is considered as a forest."
Isaiah 32:15

"And I will give them one heart, and put a new spirit within them. And I will take the heart of stone out of their flesh and give them a heart of flesh."
Ezekiel 11:19

"It will come about after this that I will pour out My Spirit on all mankind; and your sons and daughters will prophesy, your old men will dream dreams, your young men will see visions."
Joel 2:28

Not only do the Scriptures of old reveal the coming and outpouring of the Holy Spirit, but also confirm the coming of the Son of God, in The Book of Zechariah. It would be the work of Jesus, the Savior, to bring all of this about. To baptize those who would believe in Him.

God has genuine loving kindness toward His children, which expresses His loyal and covenantal love to them. When Jesus died on the Cross for our sins, all barriers between people and God were broken. All authority had been given to Jesus in heaven and on earth. The great veil of separation tore, allowing us into God's presence. Into the Holy of Holies.

Since He'd soon be at the Father's right hand, Jesus made certain that the work He came to do would continue through His people by the guidance of the Holy Spirit. His clarion call for evangelism.

Time to Weigh In

How would you describe the Holy Spirit in your own words?

Have you ever sensed the presence of the Holy Spirit?

If so, what was it like for you?

What inspired you to read this book about the Holy Spirit and His gifting to you?

Go back to page twenty-five and read once again Ezekiel 11:19. How would you interpret the meaning of this Scripture to a new believer?

Time to Grow

What are some ways in which you have experienced the Holy Spirit in your life?

Have you ever yielded to the prompting of the Holy Spirit?

If so, what was it like for you?

Are you willing to be used by the Holy Spirit?

If so, for what reasons are you willing?

2

The Holy Spirit's Purpose

"But when He, the Spirit of truth, comes, He will guide you into all the truth; for He will not speak on His own initiative, but whatever He hears, He will speak; and He will disclose to you what is to come. He shall glorify Me, for He shall take of Mine and shall disclose it to you. All things that the Father has are Mine; therefore, I said that He takes of Mine and will disclose it to you."

John 16:13–15

There are many facets of purpose and they manifest in various ways. One of those facets is that the Holy Spirit is our teacher. He teaches us the Word of God and interprets it for us. He also will guide us in the direction in which we should go.

He is a Discerner of truth. He is holy, which in the Greek is *hagios*. This means without sin, set apart. God is the holiest of all, therefore, His Spirit is the holiest of all. But how do we find out more about these facets of purpose on our own? It's not as hard as we think. Here's the good news:

WE NEED NOT LOOK TO ANYTHING
OR ANYONE ELSE FOR THE HELP WE NEED
IN MINISTERING TO PEOPLE,
OTHER THAN THE HOLY SPIRIT.

The Holy Spirit is affirmed as divine. He is:

- Called God:

  "But Peter said, 'Ananias, why has Satan filled your heart to lie to the Holy Spirit and to keep back some of the price of the land? While it remained unsold, did it not remain your own? And after it was sold, was it not under your control? Why is it that you have conceived this deed in your heart? You have not lied to men but to God.'"

  Acts 5:3–4

- Creator:

  "The earth was formless and void, and darkness was over the surface of the deep, and the Spirit of God was moving over the surface of the waters."

  Genesis 1:2

- Eternal:

  "How much more will the blood of Christ, who through the eternal Spirit offered Himself without blemish to God, cleanse your conscience from dead works to serve the living God?"

  Hebrews 9:14

THE HOLY SPIRIT'S PURPOSE

- Joined with the Father and the Son:

    "Go therefore and make disciples of all the nations, baptizing them in the name of the Father and the Son and the Holy Spirit."
    Matthew 28:19

    And...

    "The grace of the Lord Jesus Christ, and the love of God, and the fellowship of the Holy Spirit, be with you all."
    2 Corinthians 13:14

- A Revelation for Us:

    "Jesus answered and said to him, 'Truly, truly, I say to you, unless one is born again he cannot see the kingdom of God.'"
    John 3:3

- Omnipotent:

    "The angel answered and said to her, "The Holy Spirit will come upon you, and the power of the Most High will overshadow you; and for that reason the holy Child shall be called the Son of God."
    Luke 1:35

- Omnipresent:

    "Where can I go from Your Spirit? Or where can I flee from Your presence? If I ascend to heaven, You are there; If I make my bed in Sheol, behold, You are there. If I take the wings of the dawn, if I dwell in the remotest part of the sea, Even there Your hand will lead me, and Your right hand will lay hold of me."
    Psalm 139:7–10

- Omniscient:

   "For to us God revealed them through the Spirit; for the Spirit searches all things, even the depths of God."
   1 Corinthians 2:10

- Sovereign:

   "There are varieties of effects, but the same God who works all things in all persons. But to each one is given the manifestation of the Spirit for the common good."
   1 Corinthians 12:6–7

The Holy Spirit conveys an abundance of fruit through His work. The ways in which He produces are endless. They bring us many powerful devices to serve with in our ministries as we set a table of blessing before others. The Holy Spirit will never leave us without the spiritual food we need.

Many Christians have asked why the Holy Spirit still has to continue its works through us. They might assume that because Jesus finished everything on the Cross, that the work of God was finished in every way as well. But there was far more work to be done. Jesus told us that we would continue His works that He started here on earth until fruition. The work would continue throughout generation to generation. And the only way in which we can accomplish that is with the help of the Holy Spirit. The greatest purpose of Jesus leaving Him with us.

The Holy Spirit is eternal and will always be at work. He seeks to find those who are willing to yield and to be used by Him. To be directed by Him. To allow Him to work through them at any time, and in any situation. By reading the Word and learning more about the Spirit of God, we will be used for His glory throughout our stay here.

The Work of the Holy Spirit

- Anoints:

    "As for you, the anointing which you received from Him abides in you, and you have no need for anyone to teach you."

    1 John 2:27a

- Baptizes:

    "'AND IT SHALL BE IN THE LAST DAYS,' God says, 'THAT I WILL POUR FORTH OF MY SPIRIT ON ALL MANKIND.'"

    Acts 2:17a

    And…

    "Therefore, having been exalted to the right hand of God, and having received from the Father the promise of the Holy Spirit, He has poured forth this which you both see and hear."

    Acts 2:33

- Bears Fruit:

    "But the fruit of the Spirit is love, joy, peace, patience, kindness, goodness, faithfulness, gentleness, self-control; against such things there is no law."

    Galatians 5:22–23

- Bears Witness:

    "The Spirit Himself testifies with our spirit that we are children of God."

    Romans 8:16

- Comforts:

   "So, the church throughout all Judea and Galilee and Samaria enjoyed peace, being built up; and going on in the fear of the Lord and in the comfort of the Holy Spirit, it continued to increase."
   Acts 9:31

- Empowers:

   "On the other hand, I am filled with power—With the Spirit of the LORD—And with justice and courage to make known to Jacob his rebellious act, even to Israel his sin."
   Micah 3:8

- Gives Discernment:

   "For to us God revealed them through the Spirit; for the Spirit searches all things, even the depths of God."
   1 Corinthians 2:10

   And...

   "Beloved, do not believe every spirit, but test the spirits to see whether they are from God, because many false prophets have gone out into the world."
   1 John 4:1

- Gives Gifts:

   "Now there are varieties of gifts, but the same Spirit. And there are varieties of ministries, and the same Lord. There are varieties of effects, but the same God who works all things in all persons."
   1Corinthians 12:4–6

- Gives Joy:

    "For the kingdom of God is not eating and drinking, but righteousness and peace and joy in the Holy Spirit."

    Romans 14:17

    And in 2 Corinthians 7:4d:

    "I am overflowing with joy in all our affliction."

- Guides:

    "But when He, the Spirit of truth, comes, He will guide you into all the truth; for He will not speak on His own initiative, but whatever He hears, He will speak; and He will disclose to you what is to come."

    John 16:13

- Helps:

    "I will ask the Father, and He will give you another Helper, that He may be with you forever; that is the Spirit of truth, whom the world cannot receive, because it does not see Him or know Him, but you know Him because He abides with you and will be in you."

    John 14:16–17

- Illuminates the Mind:

    "For this reason, I too, having heard of the faith...Do not cease giving thanks for you, while making mention of you in my prayers; that the God of our Lord Jesus Christ, the Father of glory, may give to you a spirit of wisdom and of revelation in the knowledge of Him. I pray that the eyes of your heart may be enlightened, so that

you may know what is the hope of His calling, what are the riches of the glory of His inheritance in the saints."

Ephesians 1:15–18

- Indwells:

"But if the Spirit of Him who raised Jesus from the dead dwells in you, He who raised Christ Jesus from the dead will also give life to your mortal bodies through His Spirit who dwells in you."

Romans 8:11

- Regenerates:

"Jesus answered, 'Truly, truly, I say to you, unless one is born of water and the Spirit he cannot enter into the kingdom of God.'"

John 3:5

- Reveals Things of God:

"Now we have received, not the spirit of the world, but the Spirit who is from God, so that we may know the things freely given to us by God, which things we also speak, not in words taught by human wisdom, but in those taught by the Spirit, combining spiritual thoughts with spiritual words."

1 Corinthians 2:12–13

- Role in Christ's Ministry

"After being baptized, Jesus came up immediately from the water; and behold, the heavens were opened, and he saw the Spirit of God descending as a dove and lighting on Him."

Matthew 3:16

And...

"Jesus, full of the Holy Spirit, returned from the Jordan and was led around by the Spirit in the wilderness."

Luke 4:1

And...

"THE SPIRIT OF THE LORD IS UPON ME, BECAUSE HE ANOINTED ME TO PREACH THE GOSPEL TO THE POOR. HE HAS SENT ME TO PROCLAIM RELEASE TO THE CAPTIVES, AND RECOVERY OF SIGHT TO THE BLIND, TO SET FREE THOSE WHO ARE OPPRESSED."

Luke 4:17–18

And...

"Who was declared the Son of God with power by the resurrection from the dead, according to the Spirit of holiness, Jesus Christ our Lord."

Romans 1:4

And...

"How much more will the blood of Christ, who through the eternal Spirit offered Himself without blemish to God, cleanse your conscience from dead works to serve the living God?"

Hebrews 9:14

- Sanctifies:

"To be a minister of Christ Jesus to the Gentiles, ministering as a priest the gospel of God, so that my offering of the Gentiles may become acceptable, sanctified by the Holy Spirit."

Romans 15:16

And...

"But we should always give thanks to God for you, brethren beloved by the Lord, because God has chosen you from the beginning for salvation through sanctification by the Spirit and faith in the truth."
2 Thessalonians 2:13

- Speaks in Scripture:

"Brethren, the Scripture had to be fulfilled, which the Holy Spirit foretold by the mouth of David concerning Judas, who became a guide to those who arrested Jesus. For he was counted among us and received his share in this ministry."
Acts 1:16–17

And...

"All Scripture is inspired by God and profitable for teaching, for reproof, for correction, for training in righteousness."
2 Timothy 3:16

Now that we've seen a scriptural illustration of who the Holy Spirit is and the ways in which He works, we can grasp the importance of asking Him to work through us. Sincerely longing for His presence in our lives.

In the next chapter, we will expound on how to receive the power of the Holy Spirit. We will learn how to apply the knowledge of who He is, and His divine role into our own personal lives. Let's invite Him in.

Time to Weigh In

Have you seen the Holy Spirit in action?

If so, did you experience peace at that time?

Did you have a revelation?

Did you sense a closeness with the Lord during and after your experience?

Time to Grow

Is there a clear picture of godly fruit in your life?

Draw an imaginary image of a fruit tree. If you could name each of the fruits, what would you name them? [Example: Patience, Kindness, Forgiveness]

If not, what are you manifesting?

Do you desire to witness the Holy Spirit in action working through you?

3

How to Receive the Holy Spirit

"And when He had said this, He breathed on them and said to them, 'Receive the Holy Spirit.'"
John 20:22

The Holy Spirit and His gifts are for today. For you and me, and for all who have an open heart to yield to Him. Try and picture this: The Lord Himself breathes on us to fill us with the Holy Spirit. The word in the Greek is *emphysaō*. God's Spirit enters into us to abide within us.

I'd like to start exploring the in-filling of the Holy Spirit with you by sharing my own personal experience. One that not only drastically changed my life, but the lives of many others as well. And to God, be all the glory.

I have written two books titled, MIRACLES, about what God has done in my life in detail. But for now, I will share in part. Bits and pieces that will hopefully project a picture of God's amazing grace. My life has been a process of recovery from the depths of darkness, that leapt into the marvelous light of healing and restoration. One that started with an explosion of profound change. The Holy Spirit has delighted me with many surprises throughout the years. And for that, I am forever grateful.

At the age of fourteen, I said a prayer in a charming Foursquare church in La Verne, California. While I prayed to receive Jesus into my heart, a sensation I had never experienced overcame me. A cleanliness within as though someone had taken a large bar of soap and scoured away the clutter that had lurked there. Black became white. Darkness became light. Peace prevailed over fear. I became aware that something supernatural from God had taken place within me.

Sadly, at that time, I hadn't anyone to disciple me. Without the knowledge or guidance necessary to go forward with this newfound faith, I soon slipped back into an area of gray. Out from under the protection of God, into the world at large. Although I had tucked the memory of that special day deep within my heart, the further I traveled from that moment, the closer I neared the same difficult life I had escaped.

In February, 1980, I moved into my new home alone. Loneliness crept into my life as never before. Would I ever get married and start a family? The possibility of a lifetime without a husband and my own children saddened me. I began to drink wine to soothe my woes. My life seemed void of purpose.

Tired of hitting walls, I came to a dead-end in the game of life as I knew it. And little did I know how much that life was about to significantly change. God came to my rescue, and helped me to re-dedicate my life to Him. Once I asked for forgiveness, and prayed for Him to be the Lord of my life, sadness escaped me, moodiness disappeared. A spring of hope shot up from the depths of my soul and watered the parched soil of my smoldering past with showers of peace. Love exploded within me as my knowledge of God heightened while I grew to know Him, His Son, and His Holy Spirit. With each morning came a new song that chimed along with God's heartbeat. The Holy Spirit within me had been ignited and I simply didn't know what that meant yet. I had no idea that the gifts from Him were about to manifest through me to help others. But soon after all of this began, I studied the Bible and prayed these Bible verses below. They opened up my mind and heart. It all became clear to me.

> *"In Him, you also, after listening to the message of truth, the gospel of your salvation—having also believed, you were sealed in Him with the Holy Spirit of promise, who is given as a pledge of our inheritance, with a view to the redemption of God's own possession, to the praise of His glory."*
>
> Ephesians 1:13–14

> *"Therefore, if anyone is in Christ, he is a new creature; the old things passed away; behold, new things have come."*
>
> 2 Corinthians 5:17

Here are some more questions about the Holy Spirit that I'd ponder at that time, and I'd like to now address:

Why do we need the Spirit of God living inside of us?

Many believers ask this question. We know that in the name of Jesus, all things can be done through prayer, so why do we need the Holy Spirit? The best answer that I can arrive with is that we are limited without Him. The power in the name of Jesus flows from the mighty Spirit of God to us and through us.

Too often we Christians try and fight battles in the flesh to no avail. We use up all of our bodily power and drain our emotions dry. At the end of the day we've run out of energy and become depleted in every way. Our own strength runs out. But with God's power in us, we can face those battles in Jesus' name. It is the Spirit of the Lord within us who brings the victory. And His anointing power continually fills us, as we yield to Him.

Another way to visualize this impartation would be to picture when God blew breath into Adam and brought forth life into his flesh. And the second Adam, Jesus, was filled with the Holy Spirit in his fleshly body during his visit here on earth. This empowered Him to fulfill His mission. Luke illustrates how Jesus was led to go into the wilderness with the help of the Holy Spirit:

> *"Jesus, full of the Holy Spirit, returned from the Jordan and was led around by the Spirit in the wilderness for forty days, being tempted by the devil."*
>
> Luke 4:1–2

If Jesus hadn't had the Holy Spirit in Him, how do you think He'd have handled those forty days of temptation? The Holy Spirit brought Him out into the wilderness to prepare Him for His ministry. Without the power of God, no one can stand up to the battles before us. Our ministries would not succeed.

Being filled with the Holy Spirit is one of the most supernatural miracles of God. And soon after Jesus arose from the dead, the disciples would also have this gift. Jesus had told His disciples to stay in Jerusalem where they would be baptized in the Holy Spirit:

"Gathering them together, He commanded them not to leave Jerusalem, but to wait for what the Father had promised, 'Which,' He said, 'you heard of from Me; for John baptized with water, but you will be baptized with the Holy Spirit not many days from now."
Acts 1:4–5

The disciples had no idea how this would all come about. But with faith, they obeyed the Lord's instructions. When that great and awesome day arrived, the words of Jesus came alive:

"When the day of Pentecost had come, they were all together in one place. And suddenly there came from heaven a noise like a violent rushing wind, and it filled the whole house where they were sitting. And there appeared to them tongues as of fire distributing themselves, and they rested on each one of them. And they were all filled with the Holy Spirit and began to speak with other tongues, as the Spirit was giving them utterance."
Acts 2:1–4

Nothing short of the miraculous. It is apparent that tongues (sometimes referred to as a heavenly or prayer language) are a sign of having had received the Holy Spirit. Again, another controversial matter. I'll share briefly of how I received tongues, then we'll look closer at the subject later on.

A few days after I had said a prayer of repentance, when I had committed my life to Christ, I received my prayer language. On my way to an interview for a television commercial, I began to sing praises to the Lord in my car. Then suddenly, a beautiful melody full of words in which I hadn't known nor had ever heard replaced the song. Nothing about it seemed strange or scary. Only peaceful and surprisingly normal.

Perhaps it came easily for me to accept the new language since my grandmother had prayed in tongues often. I knew that I wanted all that God had for me. And He blessed me with my heart's desires. Once I'd been empowered by the Holy Spirit, my prayer life changed. My walk with God enhanced. A peace filtered through my mind and traveled down to the floor of my soul. I was complete. Whole. I was right where I should be—with the very life of God inside of me.

To my surprise, prophecy would come forth from my lips, along with wisdom and knowledge. I had visions and dreams. I laid my hands on the sick in Jesus' name and they recovered supernaturally. I couldn't understand God's generosity toward me. But I inadvertently refrained from asking Him about it. Without a questionable doubt, I hadn't done anything to deserve these gifts. Certainly, I had never been better than anyone else. But my love and trust in God enabled me to just accept all that I'd received with jubilance.

The Holy Spirit is the key to our becoming a new creature. Nothing else has that kind of power to change us completely into a different person. One full of God's love and anointing. With His help we can develop the mind of Christ and learn His ways. We can become a new person in Christ.

At the age of fourteen, I hadn't the maturity to receive the fullness of the Holy Spirit. Let alone understand it. Still in my rebellious years, without a desire to become obedient to the God that I had just personally met. But at the age of twenty-eight, with a weighty bundle of pain and burdens on my shoulders, change became necessary. I readied myself for that change and the commitment that came along with it.

Remember, the Holy Spirit is a true Gentleman. One who waits to be invited to move in and start up His supernatural manifestations. To bring forth the gifts He desires to give us, to work through us, to reach others.

But how do we invite the Holy Spirit to live in us?

Before Jesus left to go to the Father, He blew His breath upon His disciples and said these following words:

"Receive the Holy Spirit."

John 20:22b

The Spirit of God immediately took up residence within their mortal bodies. They hadn't questioned the act of this supernatural happening, nor did they fear it. But they received that deposit of the Holy Spirit that comes to all who believe. Later, the Apostle Paul confirmed that the Lord lives within us:

"Test yourselves to see if you are in the faith; examine yourselves! Or do you not recognize this about yourselves, that Jesus Christ is in you?"

2 Corinthians 13:5

Today, we might be prayed over by a pastor, teacher, or any member of the Body who is anointed, to be baptized in the Holy Spirit. Some people are afraid of such a thing. But think of it this way: God is spirit. He lived in temples and in the Ark of the

Covenant. He now lives in us. How wonderful. How special. How very generous of God.

> *"Do you not know that you are a temple of God and that the Spirit of God dwells in you?"*
> 1 Corinthians 3:16–17

The Apostle Paul longed to pray over others to receive the Holy Spirit. His desire was that all believers would have His power.

> *"For I long to see you so that I may impart some spiritual gift to you, that you may be established."*
> Romans 1:11

There is power in the Holy Spirit. Our faith and our speech should not be found in human wisdom, but in God's wisdom through the Holy Spirit. Let's take a look at 2 Corinthians 4:7:

> *"But we have this treasure in earthen vessels, so that the surpassing greatness of the power will be of God and not from ourselves."*

It is my belief that Christians are blessed with God's Spirit upon accepting Jesus Christ as their Lord. It's up to each one individually to use that power or not. We can accept the power of God's Spirit and use it for His glory. But we have to get it started up. Let me give you an example of what that looks like—to kindle the fire of the Holy Spirit within you:

Picture a table with a glass of water placed upon it. Floating in the glass of water is a packet of Alka Seltzer. The glass represents you. Inside the glass is water—the living water of God. And the Alka Seltzer—the power of the Holy Spirit.

If you leave the package intact, it just stays there, but there is no action. If the packet is opened, the Alka Seltzer is released to flow through every part of the water, bubbling, fizzing, and ready to take-action and be used.

The same with the Holy Spirit. If you yield to the Spirit and kindle the flame, the power of God is released within you. You are now equipped with that power, which allows God to bless you with supernatural gifts.

At times it is our own fears or disbeliefs that will hold us back from having this power. A fear of what people will think of us. A disbelief that has convinced us that the Holy Spirit only existed in the old days, and is not for today. Another obstacle that could block our understanding might be a lack of knowledge of who the Holy Spirit is. So, we shy away.

Upon being filled with the Holy Spirit, I became a new creature in Christ. My old woman passed away, and a new woman developed. After time, I became a little dry and in need of more of God's Holy Spirit power. Just like the Alka Seltzer loses its fizzle. When this occurred, I would ask God once again for another filling.

Think of it as our nutrition. After the lunch we eat is digested, we start to get hungry for dinner. The same with the Spirit of God who lives inside of us. We need to live in a constant state of renewal in the Holy Spirit daily by nurturing this precious character of God graciously living within us. There are three components in accomplishing this:

(1) Staying Grounded in His Word:

"Let the word of Christ richly dwell within you, with all wisdom teaching and admonishing one another with psalms and hymns."
Colossians 3:16a

(2) Remaining in Fellowship:

> *"Day by day continuing with one mind in the temple, and breaking bread from house to house, they were taking their meals together with gladness and sincerity of heart."*
>
> Acts 2:46

(3) Having a Faithful Prayer Life:

> *"Pray without ceasing."*
>
> 1 Thessalonians 5:17

And there are two components that are essential for moving in the Holy Spirit of God. Let's remember that if we try and move in the gifts in the flesh, we will fail:

(1) Gaining Wisdom:

> *"But the wisdom from above is first pure, then peaceable, gentle, reasonable, full of mercy and good fruits, unwavering, without hypocrisy."*
>
> James 3:17

(2) Never Grieving Him:

> *"Do not grieve the Holy Spirit of God, by whom you were sealed for the day of redemption."*
>
> Ephesians 4:30

Why do we need to continually be renewed by the Holy Spirit?

I've asked that question many times. I found the answer in the Bible. Let's look at two Scriptures. One declares a necessity to be renewed, and the other tells of the importance of the Holy Spirit's role in our redemption:

> *"He saved us, not on the basis of deeds which we have done in righteousness, but according to His mercy, by the washing of regeneration and renewing by the Holy Spirit, whom He poured out upon us richly through Jesus Christ our Savior."*
>
> Titus 3:5–6

As we are continually renewed by the Holy Spirit, we discover, develop, and deploy our spiritual gifts.

> *"Do not neglect the spiritual gift within you, which was bestowed on you through prophetic utterance with the laying on of hands by the presbytery."*
>
> 1 Timothy 4:14

Once I had received the Holy Spirit, my life changed in a monumental way. All things were new. A great peace remained in my heart. I had godly thoughts. I developed love for others that I'd never experienced before. And my love for God enhanced greatly. He has changed my whole life for good. I pray He has done so for you as well. And if not yet, soon.

Time to Weigh In

Have you been baptized in the Holy Spirit? Along with your answer, share of what you think this means, and how it is to affect a believer's life.

If so, tell about your experience. If not, explain of why you might not have been baptized as of yet:

Is there a particular Scripture in this chapter that made it easier for you to understand the Holy Spirit baptism?

If you haven't been baptized, how would you go about it? Would you be willing to share with another how to be baptized in the Holy Spirit?

Time to Grow

What attracts you the most about having the Holy Spirit living within you?

Do you earnestly desire the gifts of the Holy Spirit?

If you have some hesitations, what are they?

4

Words of Wisdom and Knowledge

"For this reason also, since the day we heard of it, we have not ceased to pray for you and to ask that you may be filled with the knowledge of His will in all spiritual wisdom and understanding, so that you will walk in a manner worthy of the Lord."

Colossians 1:9–10

Now that we've discussed who the Holy Spirit is and how to receive Him, we can dive into the remarkable manifestations that come from the gifts.

When I allowed the Holy Spirit to live inside of me, He placed gifts within me, some of which were unfamiliar. The only reason I can imagine why He gave me gifts, is that I yielded to Him, and earnestly longed to be used by Him. No matter what the cost. Later I would find a Scripture that tells us to yearn for those gifts in 1 Corinthians 12:31:

"But earnestly desire the greater gifts."

I hadn't been thinking of gifts at the time I received them. Just my zeal to serve God and to do whatever He'd ask. Little did I know that He would answer my request to serve Him in such a unique way. Numerous times the Lord used me to prophesy; to heal others by the laying on of hands and prayer; to speak forth wisdom and knowledge and words of encouragement; and to perform miracles. He has given me dreams and visions to show me upcoming events and how to go about facing them.

Please keep in mind that I am an ordinary person, not a theologian, not a scholar, but one who has been used by God with the gifts of the Holy Spirit. I guess you could say that I've had hands-on experience. I've been humbled by the way that God has gifted and used me. Believe me, we will all be satisfied to be dressed in God's clothing, prepared with spiritual gifts for the spiritual battles that lie ahead. And the more gifted Christians there are, the better. All the way around.

Below are the supernatural gifts of the Holy Spirit listed in:
1 Corinthians, Chapter 12:

1. The word of wisdom
2. The word of knowledge
3. Faith
4. Gifts of healing
5. The effecting of miracles
6. Prophecy
7. Discerning of spirits
8. Various kinds of tongues
9. The interpretation of tongues

Why don't we go through the gifts, one by one, in the order in which they are listed in the Bible throughout this and the upcoming chapters?

The Word of Wisdom

Wisdom is anything but shy. She calls out to as many who will hear her. Asking believers to come and listen to her speak of outstanding things. Words that are more costly than any earthly matter or any amount of gold. Words that will change our lives in enormous volume. To be wise in the Greek is *lābab*.

There are two different ways to receive wisdom. From the natural—which is earthly wisdom, and from above—which is good and godly wisdom. Wisdom is trustworthy. Her mouth only speaks truth. We will never hear an abominable thing come forth from her. All of her words are righteous. She will not lead us astray, but will watch over us with her direction and guidance. And she does so abundantly.

If we want to have power and authority, we need to acquire wisdom. But before we receive wisdom, we must come to God. Acknowledging that He is at the top of our list of loved ones, and that we serve Him only. It is important to follow God and His ways. He hates pride, arrogance, evil behavior, and perverse speech. Since wisdom only speaks the truth with eloquent speech, we can't go wrong by listening to her.

Some Christians are given divine wisdom, and others are to live wisely. Three Scriptures that point to this way of living are:

> *"For the report of your obedience has reached to all; therefore, I am rejoicing over you, but I want you to be wise in what is good and innocent in what is evil."*
>
> Romans 16:19

> *"Therefore, be careful how you walk, not as unwise men but as wise, making the most of your time, because the days are evil."*
>
> Ephesians 5:15–16

"Conduct yourselves with wisdom toward outsiders, making the most of the opportunity."
Colossians 4:5

These are food for thought. Nourishing guidelines for our behavior as followers of Christ. There is another type of wisdom. One that surfaces as supreme. The word of wisdom, given by the Holy Spirit. The gift that silences the ignorance of foolish men. One that we are instructed to ask for and value.

The real essence of wisdom is spiritual, and comes directly from the living God to us through the Holy Spirit:

"For the Lord gives wisdom: From His mouth come knowledge and understanding."
Proverbs 2:6

We see three words grouped together in several parts of the Bible: wisdom, knowledge, and understanding. They blend with one another for the common good of humankind.

In chapter two, of The Book of Proverbs, we are shown many things about the character of wisdom. I will showcase a few of these facets below:

1. She gives us:
   Understanding and discernment

2. She is:
   Like a hidden treasure
   A shield for us

3. She preserves us in our way

4. She delivers us

Proverbs, chapter four, tells of many beautiful gifts that come along with wisdom. Here is a list of some of them:

1. Good doctrine
2. Promotion
3. Honor
4. Grace
5. Glory
6. Many years of life
7. Good health
8. Establishment of our ways

Authentic, godly wisdom will deliver to us decisiveness and direction. She will teach us how to win souls, the importance of obedience, and to make wise choices. We need Her, and She waits at the gate of our hearts to come in and dwell.

Here's a wonderful description of wisdom, found in Romans:

"Oh, the depth of the riches both of the wisdom and knowledge of God! How unsearchable are His judgments and unfathomable His ways!"

Romans 11:33

Again, we see wisdom paired with knowledge. If you are gifted with words of wisdom, mostly everyone in your life will know you as one who excels in insight and judgment. As one with the ability to discern others' behavior and actions. And one that can see deeply into relationships.

A person with this gift would be a good counselor, contributing sound advice, while being led by the Holy Spirit.

Every believer should pray for wisdom. It is better than weapons of war. God wants His children to attain wisdom to be prepared. And if we lack it, we must ask for it.

"But if any of you lacks wisdom, let him ask of God, who gives to all generously and without reproach, and it will be given to him."

James 1:5

The Word of Knowledge

We all acquire earthly knowledge. But God's gift of the word of knowledge is anointed and more insightful than we can plainly see. His knowledge gives us clarity, conviction, and assurance of faith. With it we have a better understanding of God, His Word, and all of the gifts He has for us.

Typically, this gift is understood as one having the ability to teach doctrine with insight and a knowing that can only come from the Holy Spirit. Having accurate revelation with Scripture, and interpreting it well. Endued with knowledge is *epistēmōn* in Greek. Or one that is skilled with knowledge. Let's look at this:

"For this reason also, since the day we heard of it, we have not ceased to pray for you and to ask that you may be filled with the knowledge of His will in all spiritual wisdom and understanding, so that you will walk in a manner worthy of the Lord, to please Him in all respects, bearing fruit in every good work and increasing in the knowledge of God; strengthened with all power, according to His glorious might, for the attaining of all steadfastness and patience; joyously giving thanks to the Father, who has qualified us to share in the inheritance of the saints in Light."

Colossians 1:9–12

When the word of knowledge is given, you'll see a multiplication and magnification of these helpful attributes come into action. The believer's knowledge of the Word will be seen in their community church, small Bible study, and prayer group, as well as family and friend gatherings. They will be pleasing God and blessing others at the same time.

Many people, including myself, have called types of prophetic utterance a word of knowledge. We will see later on in the description of the gift of prophecy how this can easily happen. For now, to make things clear and easy to comprehend, let's separate the two.

This gift isn't a mystery. Once we receive Jesus as our Lord and Savior, our ears become open to the knowledge of the Holy Spirit, who also blesses us with spiritual eyes to see more clearly. To have divine understanding which gives us revelation.

"The fear of the Lord is the beginning of knowledge; Fools despise wisdom and instruction."

Proverbs 1:7

When we open our hearts to God, we also invite wisdom and instruction in—which accompany knowledge.

"Wise men store up knowledge, but with the mouth of the foolish, ruin is at hand."

Proverbs 10:14

As we receive wisdom from the Holy Spirit, we realize how important knowledge is, and how they work hand-in-hand. The Bible clearly speaks numerous times of how it isn't good for a person to be without knowledge.

I believe that God's knowledge is omniscient. He truly knows all things, including the secrets of our hearts. This is where prophecy can easily be called a word of knowledge. If God knows the secrets of our hearts, and by our having God's knowledge living inside of us, we may be shown someone else's secret. But always for good, never for evil. Even if the word is a warning.

To give you an example of this, I will share of a time when this rang true in my ministry. God had given me a "knowing," and a prophetic utterance about a Christian sister of mine. That she entangled herself into having an adulterous affair.

At first I hesitated to share this with her. What if I were wrong? But as time went by, the Holy Spirit reminded me to confront her with a warning. So I did with gentleness and love. Thankfully, she handled it well by confessing the sin, and then sincerely repenting of it.

You could call this a word of knowledge, but I prefer to call it a prophetic utterance. It is good to understand all of the gifts individually, and yet to see them all working together.

God also knows all things of the past, present, and future. Exactly why He is called omniscient. He has a personal interest in our lives which in-turn should give us a personal interest in His Spirit. To recognize the ways in which He ministers.

There is caution in the fact that this gift can be misused. Paul warns us that we can easily get puffed up with knowledge. This is why it is vitally important to remember where the gifts come from and to continually give God all of the glory. To use this anointed gift for Christian growth and maturity.

Jesus' knowledge of the Father consists of His hearing God's Word and obediently expressing it to the world. And since Jesus commanded us to preach the gospel and to continue the work that He had started, then we must also hear God's voice and share it with others. As much as we have opportunity.

Upon being born-again, I had revelation into the Word of God as never before. The Scriptures would shout out to me with understanding while I fervently studied them. I'm thankful that we have a God who gives us all that we need to grow into His likeness, and to grow His kingdom.

WORDS OF WISDOM AND KNOWLEDGE

The first church I attended recognized my gifting right away. The assistant pastor asked me to meet with him at a woman's home to pray for her. As we were praying, the Lord gave me a Scripture for her. Once I spoke the Scripture, the pastor turned to me and said, "How did you know that? There could be no Scripture in the entire Bible that would have been more significant to the situation this woman is in."

I looked at him and answered, "I don't know what the Scripture reads. God just gave it to me to give to her."

God knew everything the woman had been going through. I knew nothing. He knew exactly what she needed to hear. So He brought forth a Scripture by the Holy Spirit through a willing vessel to touch her. And it did. Not only did this experience build up her faith, but mine as well.

How many times have we overlooked this gift? Have you ever had a word that you weren't sure if you should share it or not? As we read further about the gift of knowledge, let's pray that God will use us time and time again with knowledge for others to bring forth revelation and healing to them. All in the name of Jesus. All for the glory of God.

Let's put some words to knowledge:

1. Knowledge is as Riches:

> *"And by knowledge the rooms are filled with all precious and pleasant riches."*
>
> Proverbs 24:4

2. Gives Strength to Men:

> *"A wise man is strong, and a man of knowledge increases power."*
>
> Proverbs 24:5

3. Is Wonderful Beyond Words:

   "Such knowledge is too wonderful for me; It is too high, I cannot attain to it."

   Psalm 139:6

4. Comes Easily:

   "A scoffer seeks wisdom and finds none, but knowledge is easy to one who has understanding."

   Proverbs 14:6

5. Is Discreet:

   "He who restrains his words has knowledge, and he who has a cool spirit is a man of understanding."

   Proverbs 17:27

6. Increases:

   "But as for you, Daniel, conceal these words and seal up the book until the end of time; many will go back and forth, and knowledge will increase."

   Daniel 12:4

7. Is Full of Love:

"If I have the gift of prophecy, and know all mysteries and all knowledge; and if I have all faith, so as to remove mountains, but do not have love, I am nothing."
                                               1 Corinthians 13:2

8. Is Full of Light:

"For God, who said, 'Light shall shine out of darkness,' is the One who has shone in our hearts to give the Light of the knowledge of the glory of God in the face of Christ."
                                               2 Corinthians 4:6

9. Is a Treasure:

"In whom are hidden all the treasures of wisdom and knowledge."
                                               Colossians 2:3

Earthly knowledge is gathered intellectually, including our own various emotions. Whereas, the actual gift of the word of knowledge is Holy Spirit imparted information.

I implore every reader to dig deep into the wealth of the Holy Spirit's knowledge and come up with words far more worthy than rubies. You can access full knowledge of God by faith. This takes us into the next gift of the Holy Spirit.

Time to Weigh In

Have you had a word of wisdom spoken to you by another believer?

If you have, write it down:

Has a believer ever had a word of knowledge for you?

If so, write it down:

Can you tell the difference between a word of wisdom and a word of knowledge?

Have you ever thought that you've had a word for someone directly from God?

If you have, did it come to you as a gentle whisper? A small voice within? An illustration, as in a picture?

Would you welcome more words from God to share with others?

Time to Grow

If you haven't already, would you feel comfortable sharing a word of wisdom or knowledge with someone?

Would you be embarrassed if you were incorrect?

5

The Gift of Faith

"Behold, as for the proud one, his soul is not right within him; But the righteous will live by his faith."
                                             Habakkuk 2:4

I love to see people with faith. All we need is a little. And that little can go a long way, as we know by hearing of faith the size of a mustard seed.

But to have the gift of faith is a true treasure. It is the very foundation to build our lives and ministries upon. Without it, we have nothing. In the Greek, faith is *pistos*; a firm persuasion, a conviction based upon hearing. An assurance.

God had to have given me faith when my doctor told me that I had become completely sterile and couldn't have children. Way before this diagnosis came about, the Lord had already shown me in dreams and visions that I would have two boys. Because of this, faith blossomed within my soul and I believed that God would heal me and give me my two sons.

But at times we need to believe without seeing. To have blind faith. Faith in what God promises is believing whether or not we see it right away. To hold on to that promise with faith until it manifests. And believe me, if it is truly from God, it will.

"Now faith is the assurance of things hoped for, the conviction of things not seen. For by it the men of old gained approval."
Hebrews 11:1–2

Our faith might be the size of the mustard seed. But as much as God can grow that small seed into a large bush, He can also use that small portion of faith within us to bring forth a harvest of delicious fruit. If we need more faith, we can pray for God to increase it:

"And the apostles said to the Lord, 'Increase our faith!'"
Luke 17:5

If the apostles hadn't hesitated to ask for more faith, then why should we? There is a significant number of Christians whom have been warned by teachers and pastors to never ask God for more faith. Some have actually said that it would be an insult to Him. Well, let's see how Jesus responded to the apostles' request:

"And the Lord said, 'If you had faith like a mustard seed, you would say to this mulberry tree, 'Be uprooted and be planted in the sea'; and it would obey you.'"
Luke 17:6

The Lord didn't scold or rebuke the apostles for asking Him for more faith. But instead, He encouraged them by saying that the amount they already have might be enough.

FAITH IS GENEROUS!

THE GIFT OF FAITH

Faith promotes the miraculous, as a mulberry tree uprooted and planted in the sea. If we exercise our gifts, we might witness God's hand move in the supernatural. Like anything else, faith requires attention. Our faith will grow as we put it into practice, and we'll see greater things happen, as our Lord spoke of.

Faith comes by hearing the Word of God. As we study the Bible, we'll draw closer to Christ, and His words will be stored in our hearts—ready to flow from us to help others. As this chain reaction begins, hopefully it will draw them nearer to God. Therefore, our work will not be in vain.

Do you have the faith to know that God will gift you with what you've already been prepared for by the Holy Spirit?

Many people have found it hard to trust enough to have faith. Perhaps they couldn't trust their own parents while growing up, which left them struggling to trust God. To have trust and confidence in God is key to having faith.

You might remember the story when Jesus said to the woman He had just healed, "Your faith has made you well." If we believe, and put our faith to work, then we will receive. I will talk more about healing when we get to that gift.

Everything comes through faith. Salvation, sanctification, purification, justification, and adoption as children of God. Our surrender to the righteousness of God, through Christ Jesus, instead of achieving righteousness alone, will bring us into an understanding of faith. It is a conviction based upon hearing.

"So faith comes from hearing, and hearing by the word of Christ."
Romans 10:17

It is impossible to have faith if we don't believe in God. Who or what can we put our faith in other than Him? Is anyone truly trustworthy outside of God? It is quite easy to trust the Lord and to accept Him when we know that He accepts us. After all, God *is* love and He accepts us with that love just the way we are. When we have experienced that unconditional love, we give faith access into our hearts. Each one of us are given a measure of faith to begin with. Our job is to continue to feed that measure and build it up into a mountain of faith in all aspects of our lives.

> *"For through the grace given to me I say to everyone among you not to think more highly of himself than he ought to think; but to think so as to have sound judgment, as God has allotted to each a measure of faith."*
>
> Romans 12:3

I've had the enormous blessing of seeing Jesus face to face. But you don't have to see Him to believe in Him. His existence is shown to us daily in multiple ways. We can sense His presence through the Holy Spirit and witness answered prayers. We know He is by our side, guiding us.

> *"For we walk by faith, not by sight."*
>
> 2 Corinthians 5:7

Faith changes our priorities in life. Since I had lived in a worldly manner for so long, after I'd received my new spiritual eyes, I could clearly differentiate the great contrast between my past and my present. I now put my faith in God and not in man. What seemed important to me before has had no influence on me once I'd experienced the goodness of the Lord. Every day has brought opportunity to care about people, helping me to put my own desires aside. But they weren't forgotten. While I watched over others, the dear Lord took care of me. He is faithful.

This wonderful, priceless gift of faith became my protection. I knew that God was a shield about me. It's important to remember that we have to fight the good fight of faith and keep it going. Like

THE GIFT OF FAITH

anything else that is living, we have to nurture it to keep it alive. Faith should be our greatest weapon in warfare.

Going back to when God healed me and gave me my children...The Lord told me at the exact moment of conception that I had conceived a child. One of the most exhilarating moments in my life. But for unknown reasons, the blood test I had taken to prove my pregnancy came back negative. The nurse called me to inform me that I wasn't pregnant.

This is when faith showed up. I had to hold onto it tightly while every lie and scheme endeavored to rip it out of my heart. The world tried to tell me that what God had told me wasn't true after all. The great joy within me was challenged by a lie. My mind started to weaken, and lean toward the negative, or even what might have appeared to be the logical and rational outcome. Eventually, it proved to be that I was indeed pregnant. God does keep His promises. And my faith grew.

That test of faith changed my life. Now when I know that I've heard from God, nothing can shake my faith. And I thank our steadfast Lord for that. This miracle of my healing helped to build and strengthen a solid faith that would remain. So when the Lord said once again that I would conceive a child, I knew that my second son would join our family soon.

The gift of faith is a true jewel to admire and keep polished at all times. It is developed and secured by the relationship we have with God through Jesus. We must fervently pray that our faith increases continually. So that when God asks us to step out in that faith, and do something the world might deem as crazy and wild, we will be ready.

I had to be ready the day my Pastor called me to ask if I could cover for him that night. It was 4:00 PM when I got the call. I would have to leave my house at 5:00 PM to get to the church on schedule. This gave me little time to put together a message, grab a bite to eat, and get ready to go.

As I sat before my computer, I prayed that God would give me the faith to get all of this done. I asked the Holy Spirit to guide me to design a message for the Bible study.

If you read Hebrews eleven, you will witness that the things of God are beyond our capability as humans. Only God can make a way for us when there is none.

There are many ways to use our faith. Here are a few:

1. We Are Saved Through Faith:

"For by grace you have been saved through faith; and that not of yourselves, it is the gift of God."

Ephesians 2:8

2. Faith Working Through Love:

"For in Christ Jesus neither circumcision nor uncircumcision means anything, but faith working through love."

Galatians 5:6

3. Unity of Faith:

"Until we all attain to the unity of the faith, and of the knowledge of the Son of God, to a mature man, to the measure of the stature which belongs to the fullness of Christ."

Ephesians 4:13

4. Faith is a Shield for Us:

> *"In addition to all, taking up the shield of faith with which you will be able to extinguish all the flaming arrows of the evil one."*
> Ephesians 6:16

5. Boldness in Our Faith:

> *"For those who have served well as deacons obtain for themselves a high standing and great confidence in the faith that is in Christ."*
> 1 Timothy 3:13

6. Walk by Faith:

> *"For we walk by faith, not by sight."*
> 2 Corinthians 5:7

7. Live by Faith:

> *"BUT MY RIGHTEOUS ONE SHALL LIVE BY FAITH;"*
> Hebrews 10:38a

8. Fight with Faith:

> *"Fight the good fight of faith; take hold of the eternal life to which you were called."*
> 1 Timothy 6:12a

9. Healed by Faith:

"This man was listening to Paul as he spoke, who, when he had fixed his gaze on him and had seen that he had faith to be made well."

Acts 14:9

10. Justified by Faith:

"Therefore, having been justified by faith, we have peace with God through our Lord Jesus Christ."

Romans 5:1

11. Preach with Faith:

"But what does it say? "THE WORD IS NEAR YOU, IN YOUR MOUTH AND IN YOUR HEART"—that is, the word of faith which we are preaching."

Romans 10:8

12. Abide in Faith:

"But now faith, hope, love, abide these three; but the greatest of these is love."

1 Corinthians 13:13

THE GIFT OF FAITH

If we show loyalty to our God, then we have faith. As we believe that He raised Jesus from the dead, our faith will also rise to each occasion that comes before us. Let's remember that if we have only a tiny seed of faith, mountains can be moved. As long as we acknowledge who is actually moving those mountains, God will perform great works through us. By trusting in God, our faith blossoms. We might not always realize the outcome of that growth, but others who remain will. And that will truly matter.

Time to Weigh In

Is it possible that you might have been given the gift of faith?

If so, how do you know this for sure?

Share a time when your faith truly came in handy:

Was the experience life changing for you considering your faith?

Has your faith become an encouragement to others?

Time to Grow

Are you content with the measure of your faith?

Would you like to see your faith grow outside of the measure you've been given?

How would you go about asking for more faith?

Do you believe that God will give you increase?

6

Gifts of Healing

"But for you who fear My name, the sun of righteousness will rise with healing in its wings."

Malachi 4:2

Oh, how I appreciate this gift! To be used by God to lay hands on another and see them healed is far from ordinary. It brings deep joy to allow the power of the Holy Spirit to work through me. I have seen many healed, and many miracles through this gift.

The Greek word for this type of healing is *iaomai;* to be healed. Made whole. Figuratively of "spiritual healing." Luke, the physician uses this word fifteen times. So many of the miracles that Jesus performed were physical healings.

The first time that I personally experienced a healing on my own body took place at age five when my grandmother prayed for me. As she did, I felt the warm, loving hand of God on my back, and received healing from that moment on. And many years later, I had the blessing of praying for others, as I watched God's hand heal them. There are some believers that I know who have been used by God to heal someone in the name of Jesus, but only once or twice in their walks with God. Others have healed many, and have the heartfelt desire to continue to do so. They are the ones who have been given the gifts of healing. They've been anointed by God with this wonderful asset.

Jesus believed in physical healing of the body. He performed many healings, but also respected doctors:

> *"It is not those who are healthy who need a physician, but those who are sick."*
>
> Matthew 9:12

I believe that God also heals people as He leads dedicated women and men of medicine into the discovery and recovery of body function. I myself have gotten well from taking medicines. Doctors, nurses, and technicians have truly found favor in my eyes. I have great respect for them.

We might see people healed quickly, or we might see them heal over time. Regardless, God is the ultimate Healer.

There are various ways to be healed in Jesus' name by the Holy Spirit of God:

1. Through Prayer:

> *"But this kind does not go out except by prayer and fasting."*
>
> Matthew 17:21

2. Laying on of Hands:

> "*Then some children were brought to Him so that He might lay His hands on them and pray; and the disciples rebuked them.*"
>
> Matthew 19:13

> "*They will pick up serpents, and if they drink any deadly poison, it will not hurt them; they will lay hands on the sick, and they will recover.*"
>
> Mark 16:18

3. Anointed with Oil:

> "*Is anyone among you sick? Then he must call for the elders of the church and they are to pray over him, anointing him with oil in the name of the Lord.*"
>
> James 5:14

4. Assured of Forgiveness of Sins:

> "*And the prayer offered in faith will restore the one who is sick, and the Lord will raise him up, and if he has committed sins, they will be forgiven him.*"
>
> James 5:15

5. Believing in Faith:

> "*Go your way. Your faith has made you well.*"
>
> Mark 10:52

Jesus taught us how to pray for healing, and to this day Christians use these methods in His name. Although, there might be controversy and different outlooks between denominations and believers of all stations, the healing is ours to receive. It is God's gift to us according to His will.

One point that I'd like to add to this is the importance and effectiveness of using Scripture in our prayers for healing. The Word of God is powerful. Here are two great verses to use:

"The Lord will sustain him on his sick bed."

And...

"Bless the Lord, O my soul, and forget none of His benefits; Who pardons all your iniquities; Who heals all your diseases."
Psalm 41:3, 103:2–3

These Scriptures are very special to me. The first one I prayed for a friend and his daughter who both had been in a devastating car accident. The chances of them making it through the night were slim. I prayed Psalm 41:3, that God would sustain them on their sickbeds. Our merciful God heard my prayer. They lived through the night and healed over time.

The other, when I prayed for a woman who waited to have a malignant brain tumor removed. On the way to see her at the hospital, I had asked God for a Scripture that I could pray over her once I arrived. As I sat by her side for hours, I waited and waited for direction from God. Then she suddenly remembered that a friend had called earlier with a Scripture for her to pray. Psalm 103:2–3. We prayed those verses together, and God brought forth her miraculous healing.

As we acknowledge that it is God and not ourselves who performs the healing through the Holy Spirit's power, we will be used by Him more and more. Being a Christian is an exciting life when filled with the Holy Spirit of God.

Seems simple, but all that we have to do is to ask God for our gifts, and He will deliver to us the ones He desires for us to operate. Hopefully, more of us will receive this powerful gift of healing. That our Lord will see our faith and stretch his loving arm full of healing power toward us, then through us to others.

It would be beneficial to memorize these two Scriptures above and use them frequently in our daily lives. As we move closer to His coming, a great window of opportunity will arise for healing prayers. And to pray-out Scriptures is very effective.

What if the person I pray for doesn't get healed? Or even worse, dies?

This concern has often held people back from praying for others. If a non-healing or death be a result after your prayers, it's not from lack of love or compassion. We already know that God *is* love. He desires to bless us in every way possible.

I'd never want to judge someone in saying that their lack of faith or lack of forgiveness for someone has stopped them from receiving God's divine healing. These two issues might actually hold back a healing, but it is not for us to judge.

I've known people with more faith than we can imagine who sadly didn't get healed—or haven't gotten healed yet. And I've witnessed many who had little faith be miraculously healed. This is exactly why I try to be careful with my words. Telling someone who has terrific faith that they don't have enough of it to be healed could damage them deeply.

There are other questions that I'd heard during my ministry and walk with the Lord. Here are some of them:

Do you pray for a healing if the person is near death?

Our hearts need to be open for however God leads us. If He desires to heal someone right before their last breath, He will do so. And perhaps through one of us, as we obey His call to use this gift. If the Holy Spirit prompts us to pray for this, we must never hold back doing so because of our fears or doubts. Or even our worry of raising hope in the one approaching death.

God is God, and we are but people. It's He that brings the healing power of His Spirit through our prayers and the laying on of hands. We must trust that He knows what's best for the person we're praying for. Perhaps it's His will to take the person home to heaven at that time. It's better to not get in the way of His awesome work, His perfect timing, and His divine acts.

Can you effectively lay hands on yourself to be healed?

I say, why not? If you twist your ankle and no one is around to lay hands on you for healing, then it seems logical to put your own hands upon your ankle and pray. God is not worried about the logistics while you suffer in pain. He wouldn't hold back His blessing because you were alone without help. After all, you aren't really alone. He is there with you. So, if you agree with His Word and pray with faith, you might be healed then and there. Not only is this sensible, it could turn out to be an amazing testimony.

There have been many occasions when I've opted to lay my hands on my own body for healing. And I've been healed many times this way. God is faithful and full of mercy.

I thought Jesus loved me, therefore, why didn't He heal me?

I can relate to this question. After delivering my second child, I became very ill. Not knowing what was wrong, I kept praying that God would heal me. After a few months, my health worsened. It took two more years for me to be correctly diagnosed with hyperthyroidism. This disease brought difficult challenges.

To think that God would allow me to become gravely ill with two small children to nurture honestly shocked me. Although I tried not to become bitter, temptation hung over my head at every labored breath.

We live in a world with disease, evil, and destruction. If we all lived in perfect health, it would be as living in heaven. At times we get discouraged when we hear of others being healed, and yet still await our own healings. We might ask ourselves if God loves them more than us. Or if we are unworthy of a healing.

Accidents take place. A tree that had been over-watered lost its hold in the ground and fell upon a child. Brakes went out in a bus because of negligence on a mechanic's part. People were killed. An elderly woman broke her hip when she tripped over some trash that someone spilled onto the sidewalk. We live in an imperfect world where things just happen.

If you have the gift of healing, it's good practice to always be sensitive to others. A friend of mine sadly spends her time in a wheelchair, without the ability to walk anymore. On several occasions, other believers have criticized her for not having the faith to be healed. Those of us that have the gift of healing should approach others with love. Never pushing them to allow you to pray over them. Never judging them on their condition. But to pray with love and confidence in knowing that it is God who heals. And He doesn't always do it in the same way for everyone.

We don't have all of the answers, but God does. If we make ourselves readily available to Him, we will see more healings, I am certain. And as we grow older and wiser in the Lord, we will become seasoned with His grace, which will enable us to make good decisions. Those that coincide with His.

Why do we have to pray in Jesus' name for a healing?

The healing power is in the name of Jesus. The name above all names. The Holy Spirit works through Him and through us once we've allowed Him in and yield to His guidance.

There are numerous questions that people ask regarding healing. I've always believed that if we step out in faith and have hope, that we can never go wrong. I encourage all believers to ask for the gifts of healing.

Time to Weigh In

Has anyone ever prayed over you for healing?

If so, were you healed?

If you weren't healed, were you disappointed in God?

If you were disappointed, has that held you back from wanting to have this gift?

Do you find yourself wanting everyone to be healthy?

Do you have great compassion on those who are sick, or physically challenged?

Time to Grow

Are you willing to wait patiently for a healing from God if it doesn't manifest immediately?

Are you in waiting for a healing now?

Do you have empathy for others who are suffering?

Do you feel moved to comfort them in some way?

Reflect on a time when you did reach out to someone in need of healing. Were you moved to pray for them?

Think of a Scripture that displays this type of compassion coming from Jesus to another. Write it down:

Do you believe that you have the heart and mind of Christ toward others who are in physical need?

Are you an affectionate person in general?

If you've prayed for others to be healed, tell of how you went about it:

7

The Effecting of Miracles

"The fact that a noteworthy miracle has taken place through them is apparent to all who live in Jerusalem, and we cannot deny it."

Acts 4:16

The gift of miracles is a marvelous gift. One that Jesus used numerous times during His time here on earth. But within the Body of Christ is a conflict. There are those who believe in miracles for today, and those who don't. Some believe that they were only performed in ancient days, as recorded in the Bible. They may never have seen or have had one. But when you've witnessed them with your own eyes, you can't help but believe.

First of all, what is a miracle? The word in Greek is *dunamis*; power to bring forth supernatural works that cannot be produced by natural agents and means. There are multiple ways a miracle can take place. I like to group miracles, signs, and wonders together. They are events that without a doubt involve a supernatural, miraculous action of God. He shows us a sense of His pervasive activity in nature, history, and people. Most miracles I've experienced have involved people. God's hand moves in the miraculous to show His great love.

The purpose of a sign is to point people to God. We love to see wonders from above, and as we do, it's not hard to give Him the glory. For an unbeliever, seeing a miracle doesn't necessarily bring them to the Lord. But God will work in that person's heart to woo them to Him. He will reveal that He alone is God. I've witnessed many salvations that came from people experiencing a miracle of God.

Having the Holy Spirit living within us gives opportunity to see God perform miracles through us. We may not have the gift of working miracles, but might be blessed to perform one in Jesus' name in our lifetimes. If we have the gift itself, then our lives are full of events that we'd never dreamed of being a part of.

But are miracles really for today?

Absolutely! Jesus commanded us to continue His works. That's why He left us the Holy Spirit. Although His time here seemed quite short, He accomplished many things. But once He left this earth to be with the Father, the work mantle fell to us. To step up and continue that work with confidence and faith.

> *"He said to them, 'Go into all the world and preach the gospel to all creation. He who has believed and has been baptized shall be saved; but he who has disbelieved shall be condemned. These signs will accompany those who have believed: in My name they will cast out demons, they will speak with new tongues; they will pick up serpents, and if they drink any deadly poison, it will not hurt them; they will lay hands on the sick, and they will recover.'"*
>
> Mark 16:15–18

When there is no earthly reason for something to change, you know that the supernatural of God has occurred. Only God can create a true miracle.

One of my favorite miracles in the Bible is found in the gospels. The multiplication of food. One special day I had the experience of watching God perform a miracle in my own home as He multiplied our food. Twenty more guests unexpectedly arrived right before Easter dinner. We had enough to feed our twelve guests until the doorbell rang.

I prayed. The obvious and natural thing to do. My husband, Peter, and I held our hands out over the food on the buffet and prayed for a multiplication of it. There had been a shortage of bread in the markets at that time. So, we had already realized that we could only offer three bite-sized rolls for each of our twelve original guests.

Our friends lined up in the kitchen as we held our breath. I watched in amazement as each one passed me with a full plate to the dining room. Four or five rolls sat atop the other food on each plate. Finally, the last guest passed me. Same. Four rolls and plenty of food. Peter still carved an endless ham.

What is the difference between a miracle and an answered prayer?

When I became born-again, many miracles occurred. My life had gone from normal into the realm of the supernatural overnight. The only reason that I didn't feel overwhelmed from the dramatic change had to do with my upbringing.

My grandmother, Ida, had read the Bible to me and talked to me about miracles throughout my early childhood. How miracles were for today as well. She witnessed the mighty hand of God miraculously heal her of polio at the age of sixteen. Her faith blessed me in ways that would eventually lead me into giving my heart and life to our Savior, Jesus.

The difference between miracles and answered prayer is slim, but significant enough that many believers ask this question. The reason they are similar, is that a miracle doesn't usually come about without prayer. When Moses lifted His arms up to God while standing at the Red Sea—as he pleaded for a way out for his people—God heard his cry and opened up the sea for them to travel through, escaping their enemies behind them. Moses prayed and God answered his prayer. Then performed a miracle.

An answered prayer might be that after praying for years, you finally get the job you had been asking for. Or get a great deal on a car that you couldn't afford at its regular price.

A miracle is an answered prayer, but is different and set apart. It is something that only God can bring to pass Himself. And whenever He performs one, we will almost always hear someone say that it had to be a miracle of God.

My own life became a ministry to draw others to see Jesus. To reinstate a faith that they might have wandered from. Or God might have used me to pray for someone simply because He had compassion on them. And since He had given me the gift, and I had made myself available, He used me to serve.

There are many other miracles that God so graciously allowed me to be a part of. Only God could have performed them. When we have lost control and have no power to intervene, God moves in and performs a miracle.

Jesus told us that we would do the things that He'd performed on this earth, which included the supernatural. Yet some people stop at miracles. It's true that they don't always happen. God answers prayers in various ways, but no one should lessen the greatness of what God does just because they are actions that we cannot bring forth in our own strength.

THE EFFECTING OF MIRACLES

When Jesus healed the blind man, others clearly knew a miracle had happened. A supernatural act of God. The woman in the Bible who had a blood flow for twelve years couldn't get help from physicians, only from God.

Why don't I have the gift of miracles?

Many people would love to have the gift of the effecting of miracles. It's hard to answer this question. Only God knows. But what I do know is that we need to have the faith to believe in miracles. Not to question them or fear them. And especially not to praise them. We are to praise the miracle Maker, not the action He performs. We all have a gift, and some of us have many. Whatever our gifts are, it's good to appreciate what we've been given and to use it faithfully.

If we all had the working of miracles, then who would prophesy? Who would have wisdom and knowledge? The important thing is to be open for what God has for us and to yield continually to the Holy Spirit. I love the way that Paul describes the gifts as a body:

> *"For even as the body is one and yet has many members, and all the members of the body, though they are many, are one body, so also is Christ. For by one Spirit we were all baptized into one body, whether Jews or Greeks, whether slaves or free, and we were all made to drink of one Spirit. For the body is not one member, but many. If the foot says, 'Because I am not a hand, I am not a part of the body,' it is not for this reason any the less a part of the body.*
>
> *And if the ear says, 'Because I am not an eye, I am not a part of the body,' it is not for this reason any the less a part of the body. If the whole body were an eye, where would the hearing be? If the*

> *whole were hearing, where would the sense of smell be? But now God has placed the members, each one of them, in the body, just as He desired. If they were all one member, where would the body be?"*
>
> 1 Corinthians 12:12–19

Not all have the same gifts, but they all work together for good. If each one had gifts of healing, then who would bring forth a word from God? If there were a message from God through the gift of tongues, who would interpret it? These gifts are given to various individuals by the Lord to enliven our gatherings and to edify believers in the Church body. They are also a testimony that might move nonbelievers toward God. There is nothing more exciting than to be in a meeting where you sense the Holy Spirit. When we see the gifts coming forth, we want to celebrate His presence. There is enormous jubilation in the revelation of God's mighty power.

When I first dedicated my life to the Lord, and received the working of miracles, elation filled my heart. But it all seemed natural to me. Supernatural things didn't present themselves as odd. It took me a while to understand why.

Once we have the baptism of the Holy Spirit, we think differently and all things flow as though they always had. We have a oneness with God, which gives us understanding of His ways.

Look at it this way: Each year on our birthdays, we don't necessarily feel older but we know that we are. When the Holy Spirit works through us, we know it's Him and not us. It happens in a natural way, but with a supernatural punch.

Without the Holy Spirit, we cannot perform miracles. We can close our eyes and wish for something to happen for days, but only

THE EFFECTING OF MIRACLES

the Holy Spirit can bring forth such incredible acts. As we yield to Him and believe, anything can occur. If we read and study the Word, we learn about God's methods and intentions. As we step out into faith and await an answer, we see our gifts manifesting in and through us. If we've been gifted with the working of miracles, we see them happen.

Let's recall some miracles in short description that Jesus performed when He dwelled among us, while remembering that He implored us to do the same works as He did. I encourage you to look up the Scriptures and read the stories in full:

John 2:1–11: Water turned to wine at a wedding in Cana when the host ran out of it for his guests. The first miracle that Jesus performed.

John 4:46–54: The son of a royal nobleman is healed. This miracle also took place in Cana. Although the official pleaded with Jesus to come and heal his beloved son, he stood amazed when Jesus proclaimed that his son had been healed. His faith enabled him to believe, and once he returned home, he saw that the miracle had indeed taken place.

John 5:1–9: A man is healed of a thirty-eight-year infirmity at the pool of Bethesda during the fall festival season in Jerusalem.

John 9:1–7: A man who had been born blind is made whole. Jesus said that this man, nor his parents, had sinned, but that the works of God should be revealed in him.

John 11:38–44: In the town of Bethany, Lazarus is resurrected after being dead and buried for four days. The miracle began the moment that Jesus said to the friends and relatives standing nearby to take away the stone from the grave of Lazarus.

John 21:1–14: Peter followed Jesus' directions, and caught an overflowing net-full of fish against all odds.

Matthew 9:27–31: Two blind men are healed.

Matthew 14:28–31: Peter walks on water on the sea near Capernaum at the command of Jesus. But once his faith wavered, he soon sank, then Jesus saved him.

Matthew 15:32–39: Jesus multiplies food to feed four thousand hungry people.

Matthew 17:24–27: A coin appears in the mouth of a fish to pay for Jesus' and Peter's temple tax.

Miracles were a witness to Jesus' deity. This had been prophesied in the Old Testament. He Himself had told John the Baptist that the proof of His being the Messiah would be when he witnessed that the blind would see and the lame would walk.

> *"When Jesus had finished giving instructions to His twelve disciples, He departed from there to teach and preach in their cities. Now when John, while imprisoned, heard of the works of Christ, he sent word by his disciples and said to Him, 'Are You the Expected One, or shall we look for someone else?' Jesus answered and said to them, 'Go and report to John what you hear and see: The blind receive sight and the lame walk, the lepers are cleansed and the deaf hear, the dead are raised up, and the poor have the Gospel preached to them.'"*
>
> Matthew 11:1–5

It's the same for each of us today. When God's children perform miracles in His name, people see the proof of Jesus as the Son of God. The Savior.

> **TO BE THE HANDS AND FEET OF JESUS IS TO BE A FOLLOWER OF HIM!**

To carry on the works of Jesus by the leading of the Holy Spirit is one of the most important things we can do. And as we do, we proclaim the living God to all around us. This is our duty.

Time to Weigh In

Do you believe in miracles?

That they happen today?

Have you ever seen or experienced one personally?

Please write about it below, and share it with others if you have. If not, share your favorite miracle from the Bible.

Perhaps you think that miracles only took place in ancient times. If you do, explain why you believe this way.

Time to Grow

If you've doubted that miracles can happen through you, are you willing to reassess your viewpoint with the help of the Holy Spirit?

What would make miracles more believable to you?

Do you relate to any of the people in the Bible who received or performed a miracle?

If you do, who are they, and why do you relate to these people?

Would a sense of unworthiness within yourself to perform something as significant as a miracle in the Lord's name hold you back?

How would you seek to change such an unworthiness? Write down a Scripture that comes to mind that would help you to accomplish this. If you can't locate a Scripture, tell of your concerns in the area of miracles. If you don't have any, and are open to receive this gift, tell the reasons why:

8

The Gift of Prophecy

"For no prophecy was ever made by an act of human will, but men moved by the Holy Spirit spoke from God."
2 Peter 1:21

This amazing gift is key to our verbal connection with God. It includes prophecy and prophetic utterances. At times I call it "knowing". It's communication from God to His children in various ways. Words, dreams, visions, and pictures from the Holy Spirit all fall within the description of prophecy.

The Greek word for prophetic utterances is *prophēteia*; the speaking forth of the mind and counsel of God. A declaration of that which cannot be known by natural means. The word, *prophētēs*, stands for a prophet of God. One who obediently speaks forth or openly of a divine message, foretelling of the purposes of God in the future. To receive and declare a word from the Lord through a direct prompting of the Holy Spirit within and through the human instrument is prophecy.

God desires to speak to His Body through us, and to declare truths to all of His children. Some of those truths are edification, declarations, proclamations, encouragements, future events, and even warnings. At times, He confirms His love for us.

Once I was born again, I received this amazing gift. Even with little understanding of it at the time, I was willing to go with it for God. Throughout the years, I've grown spiritually by watching God communicate with others. It's humbling to be used by God in this way. I pray that all believers covet this gift.

What is the difference between prophecy and the gift of prophecy?

Prophecy is something that every believer should seek for. It is all communication directly from and with God. To deliver a message from God's mouth to another's ears is the utmost blessing. To be a true messenger of God. And one that directly blesses others in the most unique way.

The gift of prophecy is when a believer frequently speaks forth the inspired and divine will and purpose of God as they receive it by the Holy Spirit. It always comes with deep and insightful meaning. A prediction of something to come whether as encouragement or a warning. Words that birth within the walls of the throne room of heaven and blossom in our hearts.

IF ONE HAS THE GIFT OF PROPHETIC UTTERANCE,
AND HAS MANY OTHER SPIRITUAL GIFTS,
THEY ARE A PROPHET.

Meaning in the noun form:

The speaking forth of the mind and divine counsel of God. Here's an example:

> *"In their case the prophecy of Isaiah is being fulfilled, which says, 'You will keep on hearing, but will not understand; You will keep on seeing, but will not perceive.'"*
>
> Matthew 13:14

Meaning in the adjective form:

Of or relating to prophecy, or proceeding from the prophet, or prophetic. Example:

> *"So, we have the prophetic word made more sure, to which you do well to pay attention as to a lamp shining in a dark place, until the day dawns and the morning star arises in your hearts."*
>
> 2 Peter 1:19

Meaning in the verb form:

To be a prophet. To prophesy. Speaking forth divine counsel. Example:

> *"And I will grant authority [give power] to my two witnesses, and they will prophesy for twelve hundred and sixty days, clothed in sackcloth."*
>
> Revelation 11:3

Can you prophesy without having the gift of prophecy?

Let's sum this up once again. Whereas prophecy is the message that comes from God; to prophesy is to obediently speak out what God has given to us by the Holy Spirit; and prophesying is an act of bringing forth prophecy. It is forth telling of an event to come, or a warning. Regardless of our gifts, all believers have the potential to bring forth prophecy as the Spirit leads them.

I believe that every believer can prophesy as God gives them utterance to speak. This is why we need to be open to whatever God gives us in and out of season in order to fulfill His will in our ministries, our churches, and small Bible studies. Words might be shared by a believer to an unbeliever as well. The gift of prophecy in a believer will be seen and used often. The believer will have the ability to use this gift often to foretell, edify, encourage, inform, warn, and rebuke.

What are the ways in which we can receive prophecy from God?

1. Words Given to the Prophet from the Holy Spirit to Speak Out to Others:

> *"And coming to us, he took Paul's belt and bound his own feet and hands, and said, 'This is what the Holy Spirit says: 'In this way the Jews at Jerusalem will bind the man who owns this belt and deliver him into the hands of the Gentiles.'"*
>
> Acts 21:11

2. From a Vision:

> *"And the Lord said to Paul in the night by a vision, 'Do not be afraid any longer, but go on speaking and do not be silent; for I am*

with you, and no man will attack you in order to harm you.'"

Acts 18:9–10a

3. From a Dream:

"When he had considered this, behold, an angel of the Lord appeared to him in a dream, saying, 'Joseph, son of David, do not be afraid to take Mary as your wife; for the Child who has been conceived in her is of the Holy Spirit.'"

Matthew 1:20–21

4. By a Knowing:

Jesus, Himself, shows us this example of prophecy:

"The woman answered and said, 'I have no husband.' Jesus said to her, 'You have correctly said, 'I have no husband'; for you have had five husbands, and the one whom you now have is not your husband; this you have said truly.'"

John 4:17–18

5. With the Interpretation of Tongues:

"By the same Spirit, and to another gifts of healing by the one Spirit, and to another the effecting of miracles, and to another prophecy, and to another the distinguishing of spirits, to another various kinds of tongues, and to another the interpretation of tongues."

1 Corinthians 12:9–10

And...

"If anyone speaks in a tongue, it should be by two or at the most three, and each in turn, and one must interpret."

1 Corinthians 14:27

How do you know for sure that you are truly hearing from God?

This is the tricky part, so I'll give a detailed answer: The process of learning how to use this gift is one of learning through mistakes and victories. It took me a while once I realized that I had been graciously given this gift to understand how to use it.

It seemed a little scary at times to bring forth a word from God in a group of people, let alone a church full of them. But the more that we use this gift, the more comfortable we are to continue to use it. As we do, we will see that the blessings are bountiful. It is important to remember to use it wisely. That we strive to not make mistakes with God's words.

Shortly after I became born-again, I received a prophetic word. While visiting a church with my parents, an anointing of God came upon all of us in a strong and mighty way. Words started to come to me. Over and over again. I felt a fire in my core and an urge to speak out the words so that the entire congregation could hear them. Small beads of sweat started forming on my forehead as I struggled with fear. Fear of wondering if it were God's will that I'd speak up. After all, what if I were wrong? I waited and waited, hoping that someone else would speak those words before me. Just as I began to burst from holding back, one of the pastors spoke out the message. He said the exact words that I had received.

I leaned toward my father's ear and whispered, "Daddy, I feel terrible! God gave me those words and I didn't speak them."

A sweet smile appeared on my dad's face as he softly said, "God revealed to you your gift. Because you didn't speak out the words He had given you, He spoke through someone else as they yielded to Him. Don't worry. The words came forth and you had confirmation of your gift."

Relief surfaced and calmed my pounding heart. Joy replaced my fear. From that time forward I knew I'd speak out God's words as He revealed them to me.

But it wasn't as easy as that. There were times when the Lord would give me words of warning for another. As much as I fought saying them, they were important to be said. One time, while risking a friendship, I obeyed the instructions of the Lord. The woman I had given the words to repented and promised God she'd change her ways. She safely carried on with her life while thanking God for His loving intervention.

I've held a Bible study and prayer group for women in my home now for thirty years as of this book's publication. Quite a while ago, a woman named Abby, who attended the group regularly, faced dialysis if she couldn't find a kidney donor. She had lost hope after weeks went by and her doctor had ordered dialysis for her. On Valentine's Day, she came to the group to tell us the disappointing news.

During the meeting while we were praying, the Lord told me to tell Abby that she will not have to go through dialysis. Again, I began to wonder if I should share the word from God. She had been angry at Him for His lack of provision of a new kidney, and didn't want to face dialysis for the remainder of her life.

Our relationship could be harmed, but if it meant a healthy and longer life for her, I'd give that concern up. I moved over across the room to where she sat, and stooped down to eye level, while speaking these words:

> "My dear friend, God has shown me
> that you will not have to have dialysis..."

Before I could go on, she raised her voice at me. Insulted and disgusted, she rebuked me for making such an insensitive proclamation. She left in a huff.

Later that day, I received a phone call from Abby's friend. With her rousing voice, she informed me that when Abby went into her doctor's office to receive her pre-dialysis package, the nurse told her the amazing news. They had a donor. The donor was Abby's college friend from many years past. The surgery would be set soon for Abby to receive her new kidney. She wouldn't have to undergo dialysis.

It isn't always easy to be used by God. There is a great cost. Your feelings will be hurt at times. Some people might call you delusional, or a false prophet if they aren't happy with the words you share with them. Even if it's good news, one may still not receive it well. But 99.9 % of the time, the words from God that I share are received with love and acceptance. Even those that come along with warnings and correction. And in-turn, God is glorified in all ways.

Here's a check list to keep us in line with God's words:

- Words we receive never contradict the Bible.
- If we don't have peace about sharing the words, then it's best to wait and pray about it before speaking them.
- For God to use us we must live in obedience to Him with the right motive to have this gift.

THE GIFT OF PROPHECY

This gift has changed my life. Personally, I'd rather make a fool of myself in the eyes of others than to miss out on bringing forth God's messages. Of course, only if I'm positive they are God's words, and not mine. I pray that this particular gift will be poured out upon all of God's children in these last days we are facing. I encourage you to pray for it now.

Time to Weigh In

Do you believe that God speaks through believers to other believers?

Have you ever been spoken to or directed by God through prophecy from another Christian?

If so, did you bear witness to the prophecy spoken to you?

Did the prophecy come true yet up to this time?

Do you believe the prophecy came from God, or that it could have been a coincidence that someone spoke truth to you?

If you've never had a word of prophecy, would you be excited to receive one?

Time to Grow

If you desire to have the gift of prophecy, please list as many reasons below as you can of why you hunger for this gift:

Are you willing to look like a fool to the world in order to step out for God by bringing forth words to others from Him?

Do you think that you've heard God's voice before in the way of prophecy?

If so, please describe the event or events:

If you do not desire this gift, write down the reasons:

9

Discerning of Spirits

"But he who is spiritual appraises all things, yet he himself is appraised by no one. For WHO HAS KNOWN THE MIND OF THE LORD, THAT HE WILL INSTRUCT HIM? But we have the mind of Christ."

1 Corinthians 2:15–16

This gift provides the God-given ability and insight to distinguish the nature of the spirit in operation. It might help us to tell true prophetic speech from a source opposed to God. Discerning of spirits might make us aware of the presence of an angel or a false prophet. Discernment in the Greek is *diakrisis*, meaning a clear discrimination, discerning, judging. Able to judge if someone is evil or of God. A believer with the gift of discerning will be able to separate a person out to investigate them spiritually.

Have you been somewhere when a stranger approached and you sensed something odd? An alarm goes off inside of you that detects something is not right? Not from God? This discernment is from the Holy Spirit. It protects us by warning us against listening to the utterance of falsehood or even demons.

One of the best examples of this gift that I have experienced personally happened many years ago while pregnant with my second child. My husband and I hosted and taught a coed Bible study at our home. We knew that a man who called himself a prophet had plans to visit our next meeting. When he did, he started having words for a few people during our prayer time.

He came over to me and unabashedly put his hands on my tummy and started to prophesy. The minute he referred to my baby as "she", I knew his words were not from God. During the previous two years, I had been shown in pictures and dreams that two sons would be born to me.

I immediately drew back and rebuked his words. Shock covered his face as I corrected him by proclaiming that God had placed a son in my womb, therefore he had not been hearing from, or speaking for God.

To my surprise, even after my intervention, he continued to talk about my daughter. I finally asked him to leave the meeting.

Time proved truthfulness in the promise I had received from God. I delivered my second son. We must never allow the enemy's or one's own thoughts to confuse or interfere with the words and promises of God.

I would strongly suggest that when we hear false words to act quickly by nipping it in the bud so-to-speak. Not allowing the lie to continue and filter into others' lives as well. Often, false prophecy can damage one's walk with God by bringing in confusion to the situation.

It's not easy to be bold, but at times we must be for the sake of our Lord and of others. Distinguishing right from wrong, good from bad, and truth from falsehood takes practice. The more that we read, study, and digest God's Word, the more discernment we will have. If we make it a habit of obeying the message of righteousness, we will mature in the faith and easily be able to distinguish good and evil.

> *"But solid food is for the mature, who because of practice have their senses trained to discern good and evil."*
>
> Hebrews 5:14

A greater challenge has presented itself in our world today. Right from wrong has been dismantled. Political correctness has risen to the top of all common sense, all knowledge of the truth, and all obedience to God.

More than ever, distinguishing of spirits is a valuable gift to ask for. As we approach these difficult days ahead, it is a great asset to utilize. The Word of God makes all these matters clear to us. Within its pages, God has given us all knowing to go forward into the darkness with the brightness of Christ. To bring that darkness to light and expose it, while being led by His Spirit.

By speaking right and godly things, God will keep us on a straight path, while securing our footsteps.

> *"The mouth of the righteous utters wisdom, and his tongue speaks justice. The law of his God is in his heart; His steps do not slip."*
>
> Psalm 37:30–31

How am I to be certain that I'm discerning correctly?

This is a great question. Have you heard the expression, "I know what I know, what I know"? There is an uneasy sense in us when we see or hear something that is not from God. And there is a peace that comes with hearing the truth. To rely on this "knowing" in consistency with Scripture is the best method.

Years ago, I had a word from God for a couple who were awaiting the birth of their first child. As I shared the word that they were going to have twins, they rebuked the very thought in order to coddle their own desires and conveniences.

God clearly gave me this precise word to prepare them for something they weren't expecting. Sadly, they reacted in the flesh. Later they informed me that after they'd prayed and brought this before the Lord, they were at peace with the prospect of having twins, and believed that this word came from God. Indeed, soon they were the parents of twins.

WHEN WE GO BEFORE OUR GOD AND PRAY THAT THE HOLY SPIRIT GIVES US DISCERNMENT, WE NEED TO LISTEN IN THE SPIRIT. IF WE REACT IN THE FLESH, WE MIGHT MISS HEARING FROM HIM, AND BE BLINDED TO THE BLESSINGS AT HAND.

Every true word one receives will comply with God's Word. Therefore, if we hear someone prophesy and we know that it contradicts the Bible, then we know the words are false.

Many years back I met a Christian couple in their forties, who had just married. They had shared with me that God told them each to divorce their Christian spouses and to marry one another. This contradicted the Word of God. Their fleshly desires were strong and overruled discernment of right and wrong.

It is good to be careful not to go against God's Word, as depicted in this Scripture:

"He who turns away his ear from listening to the law, even his prayer is an abomination."

Proverbs 28:9

Every church needs this gift within their body of believers for the ability to distinguish the works of God from demonic activity. So often someone slips into a congregation of believers to bring destructive words and guidance. These people are called wolves in sheep's clothing.

> *"Beware of the false prophets, who come to you in sheep's clothing, but inwardly are ravenous wolves."*
> Matthew 7:15

It makes sense that the devil would mingle in the Body of Christ, disguised as a believer to bring forth destruction. He's clever and sneaky, which is why this gift is so valuable.

Here's a list of ways in which to discern right from wrong, and good from evil:

1. We know them by their fruit. Is the person bringing good things into the church? How is their lifestyle?

2. Are their words true according to the Word of God and the Scriptures?

3. Do we have peace while hearing them speak supposed words from God?

4. Do they use Scripture for their own purposes of deceit?

5. Will a word they present to you bring you closer to God, or further from Him?

We must also have discernment within the daily decisions we make as believers. As impossible as this might be to imagine, each of our words should be carefully orchestrated. If we aren't certain that we're discerning correctly, then we can ask another member in our church who has the gift of discerning of spirits for their godly opinion. Remember, as the Scripture says, in the multitude of counselors there is wisdom. And iron sharpens iron.

The wonderful presence of the Holy Spirit is essential for a healthy church and our own personal prayer lives. For our families, small group studies, and communities as well. A beneficial blessing it will be as fellowships grow from this gift.

Time to Weigh In

During your walk with the Lord, have you ever sensed bad spirits? Maybe at an event or around other people?

If so, write down one example:

Have you ever had fear of the unknown in the spiritual realm?

Do demons and evil acts make you afraid?

If so, in what ways?

Time to Grow

If an experience with demons or an act of evil has given you fear, please bring it to light by sharing the event with your group, or another Christian.

Are you aware that greater is Jesus in you, than he (the devil) that is in the world? And that you can do all things through Christ Jesus who strengthens you?

Are you willing to be used by God to see in the spiritual realm for the good of you and of others?

10

Tongues—
The Heavenly Language

"And these signs will accompany those who have believed: in My name they will cast out demons, they will speak with new tongues."

Mark 16:17

The act of speaking in tongues, which I call heavenly or prayer language, might be the most controversial manifestation of the Holy Spirit among Christian denominations. To me, it is one of the most natural. The very thing that confirms the Holy Spirit's residence within us.

The word in Greek for tongues is *glōssa*; "like as of fire" at Pentecost. The supernatural gift of speaking in another language without its having been learned or known. An unfamiliar verbiage that can be interpreted by one with the gift of the interpretation of tongues. This gift is used in churches at times if God chooses to speak to His people in this manner. The Holy Spirit will give someone with the gift of tongues a divine message that another with the gift of interpretation will deliver. There are various types of tongues. Prayer language, tongues that bring prophecy, and tongues that bring forth the interpretation.

To make the gifts more clear, let's first begin by looking at the language itself:

Speaking in Tongues

We might have heard adults praying in another language while growing up in church. Some of us have stumbled upon this unique present from the Holy Spirit on our own. I first heard my grandmother speak in tongues when I was age five.

Tongues are a gift from God and quite a supernatural one, indeed. We can all speak in tongues even without the gift of tongues. God gives us a new language to pray with, but also as a gift to some to be interpreted.

I believe that if one is baptized with the Holy Spirit, that they automatically receive their prayer language. They might not use it, or even realize that it's there. After some time, the language may present itself while in worship. Whether singing, praying, or meditating on the Word. If it is welcomed, it will come alive.

THE SAME WITH THE HOLY SPIRIT—UNTIL WE KINDLE THAT FIRE, THE GIFTS THAT GOD HAS GIVEN TO EACH OF US ARE QUIETLY AWAITING THEIR INVITATION TO MANIFEST FROM WITHIN US.

There are a variety of Christian denominations that hold tight to their belief that tongues are not for today. They run around the Scriptures to somehow stifle the life of tongues, and yet allow other gifts that are listed alongside tongues to flow freely. Some go so far as to say that tongues are of the devil. I fear for those who say this. It is blasphemy to do so.

To further explore this beautiful manifestation of the Holy Spirit, here are some widely known questions to ponder:

How do I know if I'm really speaking in tongues?

Here are three solid answers to that question:

1. If we have received Jesus Christ into our hearts as our Lord and Savior, then begin to speak in another language while in prayer.

2. If we don't understand the language in which we are speaking.

3. If we feel closer to God while using our prayer language and have revelation of things in the Spirit.

It is profoundly important for us to have charity of heart as we minister unto others. Love always prevails. We need to know the Scriptures and its proper order about tongues. If we go to church and start speaking in tongues and do not have love, it becomes an annoyance to others:

> *"Though I speak with the tongues of men and of angels, but have not love, I have become sounding brass or a clanging cymbal."*
> 1 Corinthians 13:1

Why does God give us a language that we can't understand?

As we speak in our prayer language, we speak mysteries to God. The devil cannot translate or understand tongues. Therefore, it is a perfect conduit to speak straight into God's ear without any other interception or distraction.

> *"For one who speaks in a tongue does not speak to men but to God; for no one understands, but in his spirit he speaks mysteries."*
> 1 Corinthians 14:2

Numerous times while I'd prayed and spoken in tongues, miracles occurred. Or God would give me a picture or a vision. Several years ago, my two prayer partners, Sarah and Jenny, came to pray with me at my art studio. As we began, I prayed in tongues, and the Lord gave me a vision. I found myself walking on a lit-up path toward Jesus, who waited at the gate for me. I couldn't take my eyes off of Him. He smiled at me, and I stood flooded with His love and acceptance.

One evening many years ago, while praying in tongues, my husband asked me to receive words from God for him. He had been frustrated with his work situation and was eager to hear direction from God. It was somewhat of a desperate plea. To my surprise, the Lord gave me an hour-long vision with prophecy. One that not only gave words and direction for Peter, but revealed things concerning world events leading up to end times.

Our prayer language is holy, anointed communication that breaks through the enemies' barriers to reach God. And once that connection is opened, anything can happen in the supernatural realm. This includes various visions, dreams, miracles, prophecies, revelations, visitations, restorations, and healings. Whatever God desires to bring forth to us to hear, visualize, and to take heed to.

Praying in the Spirit is praying in tongues. We don't know what we are saying, but God does, and speedily answers us. It's our hotline to God. What believer wouldn't want that?

> *"But you, beloved, building yourselves up on your most holy faith, praying in the Holy Spirit, keep yourselves in the love of God, waiting anxiously for the mercy of our Lord Jesus Christ to eternal life."*
>
> Jude 1:20–21

If we want a direct line to God, then we need to ask for Him to make manifest the hidden language deep within us that He lovingly planted. As the fire of the Holy Spirit rises up, the words will flow like living water. And a beautiful language that we've never spoken before will come forth from our lips to God's ears.

Some believers only want certain parts of what God has to offer to them. And there are those who want it all. I believe I would be included in the latter group. How about you? Everything that God has to offer us is good.

Why does this language have to be called *tongues*?

I have asked this question myself. The Greek term *glossa* means "tongue" or "language." On the Day of Pentecost, when the believers were first empowered with the Holy Spirit, they spoke in many languages. This occurred so that those from far countries who had gathered together could hear the message in their own language. Their own native tongue.

The Gift of Tongues
and
The Interpretation of Tongues

This is part two of the mysteries of tongues. The part that brings forth prophecy from God with the help of two believers. Whereas one believer prays aloud in tongues, another interprets the message for the congregation. An expression of the mind of God for the instruction of the Church.

If you have the gift of tongues for prophecy, there will be another believer with the gift of the interpretation of tongues in your group or church. It is common that tongues will be spoken by a few believers, then one interpretation will come forth from the gifted interpreter.

Neither party knows what every individual word means in the language of tongues. The interpreter receives the meaning of the words by the Holy Spirit to speak to the Body. This usually happens in church, or during a prayer meeting, or a convention, or revival meeting. Wherever the believers gather together to praise, worship, and to seek God. Although, I have experienced this in a one-on-one setting. And, surprisingly, have discovered that one believer might pray in tongues, then interpret it.

ONE BELIEVER MAY HAVE BOTH GIFTS. TONGUES AND THE INTERPRETATION OF TONGUES.

"Therefore, let one who speaks in a tongue pray that he may interpret. For if I pray in a tongue, my spirit prays, but my mind is unfruitful. What is the outcome then? I will pray with the spirit and I will pray with the mind also; I will sing with the spirit and I will sing with the mind also."

1 Corinthians 14:13–15

Once, while praying at the kitchen table, my friend spoke in tongues. I then received the interpretation. Another time, I spoke in tongues then received the interpretation myself. To think that our God speaks directly to us in this way is very exciting.

It is also wonderful when in church someone speaks out in tongues, then another interprets it. The whole congregation gets blessed with a special message from God as well as unbelievers who are in the church. They can witness firsthand the words coming forth from God.

Does there always have to be an interpretation of tongues?

In a fairly large church or gathering, people are normally uncomfortable hearing languages they don't understand, so Paul had urged the believers to pray for interpreters when tongues are spoken so that the whole church would benefit from the message.

I agree that in church we should speak in our normal language so that all can comprehend the message from God. But at times, the Lord will bring His own personal message to the group through the speaking of tongues—and the interpretation of those tongues that follow.

All believers are exhorted to seek these gifts in order to build up the Church. They are valuable instruments for us to use.

Time to Weigh In

Have you ever been told that this gift is from the devil, or that it is not from God?

If you have, how do you believe that you can overcome past statements that might have held you back from receiving this gift?

Time to Grow

If you have the gift of tongues, do you use it?

Would you be open to God using you to deliver a message to the Body in the future?

Why do you suppose this gift is important to God?

11

Ordinary People

"So that the man of God may be adequate, equipped for every good work."

2 Timothy 3:17

All of the believers that I know personally who use the gifts of the Holy Spirit are normal, ordinary, and imperfect people. This means that you and I are able to move in these precious gifts of God for the furthering and growth of the Body of Christ.

By doing so, we might be mistaken as being pompous or having spiritual pride, thinking we are better than others. But as long as we know that God is doing the work through us, and we use our gifts with love and the right motive, then it shouldn't stop us. The enemy will try and use other believers to criticize and accuse us so that we won't continue to move in the Holy Spirit. We must not allow this to steal our joy in serving God.

All fear is gone when we understand the spiritual warfare at hand. But let us know and be at peace with the knowledge of God's Word and His commands to us as His children. We are to do the works that He left for us to do. To minister the gospel all over the world. To heal the sick and lame. To raise the dead. Yes, even that! Anything that Jesus did, we can do now because we have God's Spirit living within us.

But how can a sinner like me be used by God in a supernatural way?

We can't help but sin now and then, but we have been forgiven of our sins through the shedding of Jesus' blood on the Cross. He died for us for this very reason. We are righteous in Christ, but within ourselves we are still sinners who have been saved by grace. This by no means should give us a green light to sin. Transgressions should be halted, as we yield to that grace.

> *"Anyone who [transgresses] and does not abide in the teaching of Christ, does not have God."*
>
> 2 John 9a

Jesus said we would do greater things in His name once He left to be with the Father in heaven. But He didn't leave us alone. He gave us the Holy Spirit. Our Helper. And now we can heal the sick and raise the dead in the name of Jesus.

Once we get over worrying about what others think of us, or might say about us—and as long as we know we are pleasing to our God—we can move mountains for Him if need be. All things are possible through Jesus Christ. And prayer with faith brings that into fruition.

So now that we understand that we're not to be embarrassed or ashamed of what God desires to do through us, I will share a few more wonderful things that the Lord has used me to do in His name. I pray that a fire within your soul kindles as you read these stories. That you will hunger to be used by God. And He alone gets all the glory. And I, none.

I'll start with the gifts of healing:

Gifts of Healing

I discovered early on in my walk with God that I had this gift. Passion grew in my heart more each day for others. The sick and the needy. I yearned to touch people. To put my hands upon them to help make them well and whole in the name of the Lord.

Out of this passion that God put in my heart, along with the power of His warm, healing touch, numerous healings have been manifest in Jesus' name. Miracle healings came forth.

From skull damage and broken ribs in a bunny rabbit—to a brain tumor in a pregnant woman—healings have come to pass before my eyes. I've never gotten tired of seeing God's power of the Holy Spirit move to help others in pain and despair. To make them whole again.

There were times when fear tried to foil my obedience when an urgent matter would arise quickly. But as I took a deep breath and got into the Spirit of God, I'd relax and become a useful vessel for Him. I trusted that all would work out as God willed.

From the time of my sons' births, throughout their teens, I'd pray with faith when they were ill or injured. God never let me down. He was by my side through it all.

One of the most difficult times for me as a mother came when my son, Stephen, was hit in the nose by another student at his school, as I watched in horror. With no time to spare, I raced him to the nearest bathroom along with two of his friends. When

Stephen looked in the mirror, we all saw a bone poking out under the skin at the bridge of his nose. The boys gasped, as I shook and started to pray. I grabbed paper towels and dampened them under the faucet. After cleaning the blood away, I began to pray for a miraculous healing. And that's when the miracle came.

The two boys, along with Stephen and I, witnessed the bone move back into place. Another gasp from all of us. We got into my car and headed for the doctor's. Stephen did have to have surgery right away, but God had spared him by moving the bone earlier. The X-Ray showed that if that bone had been a fraction of an inch closer to his brain, Stephen could have died.

If an ordinary mother can bring forth healings in Jesus' name, than you can as well. Each of us can be used by God now and then for bringing forth healings. When we have been given the gift, as we yield to the Holy Spirit, we witness a great number of divine healings.

As we remember that the Holy Spirit is supernatural, then anything that can't be done in the natural can be done by and through Him.

Prophecy

When I first committed my life to God, I had many gifts that I really didn't know what to do with. But as time went by, I learned how to use them in orderly, proper ways.

As mentioned before, I have something that I call knowing. It is part of the gift of prophecy. At times, a slight impression so subtle that it could have easily escaped me. I would have a thought about my car. That perhaps it had something wrong with it. That day I would get a flat tire. After being angry with myself for not listening to that small quiet voice within, I counted it as a learning experience.

We all make mistakes along the way, but somehow learn with these mistakes. The Lord is merciful and will reveal to us more than once the things He wants us to know.

The next time I had a vague thought, I took it seriously. The Lord would always make things clear and confirm with me that He had been the One showing me the signs or impressions for my own safety.

During my Bible study and prayer meetings, the Lord has given me words for others. One example, the time when a new woman came to my prayer group. I had no knowledge of her background, not even where she lived.

As we were in prayer, the Lord had me say these words to her: "Darla, what does the Red Cross mean to you?"

She looked at me with great surprise and asked me why I would ask her that.

I answered, "Because the Lord is showing me that you are somehow involved. And He wants to encourage you to keep working there. He's going to give you more responsibility and use you in wonderful ways."

Her jaw dropped as she spoke: "I work for the Red Cross and I know that you wouldn't know that. I've been considering leaving, but now I know not to."

Darla saw the Holy Spirit's work in her life that day. Only He could have known all the things that He gave me to say to her.

Expressions from God came at nearly every study. Countless words of encouragement, direction, and warnings came forth through me while being led by the Holy Spirit. Whatever God brought my way, I took seriously. To watch God minister to His children while using me as His servant truly blessed my life and ministry. The very thought of it all humbles me.

A few marriages were saved because of this gift. A great number of people were healed physically, emotionally, and spiritually. Great and marvelous things came about by the mighty hand of God.

On other occasions, God would give me prophecy for others in group meetings and in church. With some words, I would wonder if I'd really heard from God. I would hear things like:

- "Ask if anyone has a sharp pain in their left ear."

- "Ask if anyone had just been hurt by their sister, who has dark hair and green eyes."

- "Ask if anyone has a father who moved far away, and is now in the hospital with pneumonia."

- "Someone here has a broken heart from a past friend whom you haven't heard from for five years until yesterday. God wants to use you to heal this relationship and bring this friend to Him."

And the craziest of all, when the Holy Spirit led me to ask a woman named Jules if she were expecting some money from Turkey. (You can imagine the nerve I had to muster up for this one.) The woman answered, yes. Then I continued: "The Lord wants you to give the money to charity when you receive it."

Jules showed astonishment on her face. Then with a slow grin, she responded: "Connie, God just reminded me through you that years ago I had promised Him that if I ever received some money from Turkey that was owed to me that I would give it all to charity. And if you hadn't been obedient to share this word to me, I would have literally lied to God. I'm so grateful!"

The whole group praised God for this unusual word. We learned a lot that day, as our guide, the Holy Spirit, taught us.

Ordinary women. Normal in every way. All loved the Father, the Son, and the Holy Spirit. And what did He do? He used us for many great things throughout the years. Separately and as a whole. A family of women who waited for His divine presence to manifest in wondrous ways. Desiring to be used by Him.

Now and then I would have a word that suggested that people repent of a particular transgression, or to forgive someone who had hurt them deeply. So many were blessed when inspiring words of encouragement came forth from God's loving heart to touch their hurting souls.

Descriptions of various illnesses, details of the workplace, marital stresses, or other problems would be brought up. Any concern of any kind that you can imagine has come forth over years of ministry. And it has been amazing to watch.

Do you see why these gifts are so necessary for the healing and edification of the Church? Not only the Church, but for unbelievers as well. Many people have received the Lord after I'd said things to them from the Holy Spirit's prompting.

The Effecting of Miracles

When there is no earthly reason for something to change, you know that the supernatural of God has occurred. He only can create a true miracle. The world might try and tell us that these "miracles" just happen. Even to say God was not involved.

One evening, a friend of mine named Cathy called me from the hospital where she laid dying of what we'd find later was Legionnaire's Disease. It had not been diagnosed at the time she called and said she'd been left to die with morphine flowing through her cold veins. She also had a whopping 107-degree temperature.

NOTHING SHORT OF A MIRACLE WOULD SAVE HER!

Immediately, I started to pray with fervency. I commanded the fever to leave her and that a correct diagnosis would come, along with a complete recovery. Later we found out that her husband left back for home that very night, after being told that his wife would be gone soon. That they couldn't do anything at all to save her.

The next morning, Cathy's husband, Nate, called me. He shouted with gratefulness that a healing had occurred. As we discussed all of the details, I found that Nate had no idea whatsoever that Cathy had called me the night before. As a matter of fact, he remained shocked when I had told him that she had. He proclaimed her comatose state and that she laid moments from death proved impossible for her to have called me. He then saw the miracle.

Clearly, one of the most outstanding miracles I'd ever witnessed. And it was one of the numerous miracles that I'd been so very blessed to be a part of. To see God heal miraculously through answered prayer. Nothing has been so fulfilling and rewarding in my entire life than experiencing these miracles.

We need more miracles in this dying world. Let's become a Body that is active in the power of the Holy Spirit!

We might be told by God that a woman with black hair is going to greet us on our walk. He may tell us her name and that she will ask us a question about the Holy Spirit.

At times we might hear the small voice inside that will direct us to someone's home to see that they had just died. Then God may guide us to lay hands on them and raise them from the dead in Jesus' name. The Lord may have us cast out a demon and witness Him miraculously heal a child who has never spoken a word. Then suddenly hear that child say his first word. I know these things still happen because I have seen God do all of these miracles before my eyes.

God uses people like you and me to accomplish great things and to perform miracles. We are all sinners, and yet He uses us in supernatural ways by His Holy Spirit. It is truly amazing to be a soldier for Christ. To see miracles manifest before our eyes. I implore you to ask for this gift. You will cherish it forever.

Time to Weigh In

How often have you been around the movement of the Holy Spirit with the gifts flowing?

If you have, did you feel comfortable?

If not, please explain why:

Time to Grow

Being that you are an ordinary person, would you be open to God ministering through you supernaturally to touch others?

If not, what would hold you back from that?

After our study together on the supernatural spiritual gifts, there's still more yet to come. The spiritual service gifts are also appointed by the Holy Spirit. Continue with me through Section Two, which holds all sorts of treasures for us! We just might find we have more gifts too!

SECTION TWO

SERVICE GIFTS OF THE HOLY SPIRIT

"Since we have gifts that differ according to the grace given to us, each of us is to exercise them accordingly: if prophecy, according to the proportion of his faith; if service, in his serving; or he who teaches, in his teaching; or he who exhorts, in his exhortation; he who gives, with liberality; he who leads, with diligence; he who shows mercy, with cheerfulness."

Romans 12:6–8

12

Many Ways to Serve

"Therefore, it says, 'WHEN HE ASCENDED ON HIGH, HE LED CAPTIVE A HOST OF CAPTIVES, AND HE GAVE GIFTS TO MEN.'"

Ephesians 4:8

More than likely, we've all been gifted with one or more of the supernatural spiritual gifts. But have we ever wondered what our service gifts are? If so, have we identified them correctly?

There are countless ways to serve our God and His Church. We may have several service gifts that we're not aware of. If we've been serving in one area, we might find that we have gifts in other service ministries as well.

The supernatural gifting of the Holy Spirit, which we went through in the first section of this book, also offers gifts to serve, edify, encourage, and bless the Body of Christ. And it doesn't stop there. Our unique and individual ministries overflow to the world at large. How do we accomplish furthering the message of salvation by using our gifts to serve one another? How can we be more aware of those who might benefit from our service? To find out, we first need to yield to the Holy Spirit and by faith receive our gifting. It takes practice to also execute our gifts properly. Once we start to use them, it becomes more natural to us.

There are endless opportunities to serve for Christ. He gives us gifts that can fit in well according to our lifestyles. If we are married, single, living in a city or the country, there is conducive work for us to do. We are ministers for Christ, able and willing to use our gifts from God to further His kingdom. These service gifts will offer us specified direction in which our ministries will flourish. Along with that will come divine instruction for the use of our gifts in our service.

By receiving Christ, we have become daughters and sons of God. Joint heirs with Jesus, Himself. We are now a family—the family of Christ. We are given special purposes and performances to benefit one another. Each believer develops their gifts over time as they faithfully practice and use them correctly in the anointing of the Holy Spirit. As we work closely with other members of the Body, our gifts intermingle, working together for the edification of all.

We must be open to this type of fellowship, by working side by side for the building up of others. Our spiritual vitality might easily be drained away through isolation. Our growth as a Christian and a member of the family of God takes place as we stay in blended ministry. We can learn to depend on one another, which is exactly what God intended for us to do.

It's wise to exercise our gifts so that they won't become dormant. A weekly local church or home meeting can benefit our walks with God. And as we serve together, we find ourselves living within a well-functioning family. Each member displaying their special gifts that both benefit and encourage other members to start up their gifts as well.

Every Christian might have one or more of the service gifts. The Holy Spirit decides what gifts to give to whom. We must trust that He is fair and knows which ones will work well through us as we yield to accept and to execute them. These gifts will serve the Body in a significant and purposeful way.

I'm thankful that we've all been given a measure of grace. But there's no limit to how many gifts we might have now or will receive soon. God will never give us more than we can handle.

The gifts might be given at the moment of our new birth in Christ, but might not be discovered for a time. Some of us recognize and practice our gifts all at once, and others might discover their gifts over a gradual process. In any manner, it's important to be open to them and to yield to them once we do discover them.

To understand the difference between fruit of the spirit gifts and the supernatural spiritual gifts, we can look at it this way: Spiritual fruit is produced from within, whereas spiritual gifts manifest through service.

- Fruit—Christ-like Character

- Spiritual Gifts—Christian Service

The fruit of the Spirit should be the context for the operation of the gifts of the Spirit. Spiritual gifts without spiritual fruit are worthless.

These gifts aren't the same as our natural talents. Sometimes our natural talents work alongside our spiritual gifts and they add a supernatural effect. All of our gifts are given to us by God. It's important to apply those gifts to God's will and work with our guide; the Holy Spirit:

> *"But I say, walk by the Spirit, and you will not carry out the desire of the flesh."*
>
> Galatians 5:16

It may be hard to comprehend the meanings and differences of spiritual and service gifts. There has been a wellspring of gifts poured out to us to utilize for God's purposes and plans.

Jesus told us that we'd continue the works that He'd begun. As we do, it will enable us to go deeper in our understanding of the gifts, as the Holy Spirit guides and teaches us. Can you think of some ways that our Lord served during His stay on earth? He was a great example to us of how to serve with love. Let's look at some of the more commonly asked questions about service gifts:

Why does God give us service gifts?

God's gifts are spiritual equipment for service and edification of the Body. When Jesus ascended, He went to be seated at the right hand of God the Father. But He didn't leave us alone. He left us the Helper, just as He had promised His disciples.

Jesus gave us the Holy Spirit and the gifts therein. He didn't leave us without the power or the equipment He knew that we'd need. He revealed His confidence in us by giving us His Spirit. He entrusts us to carry on the work of the Father in His name:

> *"Whoever speaks, is to do so as one who is speaking the utterances of God; whoever serves is to do so as one who is serving by the strength which God supplies; so that in all things God may be glorified through Jesus Christ, to whom belongs the glory and dominion forever and ever. Amen."*
>
> 1 Peter 4:11

What's the difference of being called to a ministry, and called to an office?

We are all called to a ministry of some sort that will glorify God, but not every believer is called to an office. The difference is that a ministry utilizes God-given gifts. Along with those gifts come opportunities for ministry. Whereas, offices are normally thought of as evangelists, teachers, elders, and deacons.

There are many believers who have spiritual gifts and use them in the church but have never had an office in the church. This is both appropriate and biblical. The distribution of various gifts to different people brings diversity to benefit the entire Body, not just the individual Christian.

"But to each one is given the manifestation of the Spirit for the common good."

1 Corinthians 12:7

What does it mean to be charismatic?

The Holy Spirit distributes spiritual gifts, sometimes called grace gifts. To be charismatic is to use those gifts by allowing the Holy Spirit to work in and through us. His work is not of ourselves, but divine and holy, and set apart.

ANY GIFT FROM ABOVE THAT IS CHARISMATIC AND UNDESERVED BY MEN IS SUPERNATURAL.

If a believer is anointed by the Holy Spirit with His gifts, they may be known as charismatic. A church that allows and invites the Holy

Spirit in to minister through its congregants in this way is usually called a charismatic church:

> *"You also, as living stones, are being built up as a spiritual house for a holy priesthood, to offer up spiritual sacrifices acceptable to God through Jesus Christ."*
>
> 1 Peter 2:5

Why do some Christians have multiple spiritual gifts, and others seemingly none?

As I've expressed before, at least one gift is given to each believer to edify the Body and to glorify God. Although this is God's desire, not all Christians are open to receiving gifts from the Holy Spirit. If a believer is found faithful and works with what God has given to them, they may receive more than one gift.

It's important that we seek the gifts in order to work with God and to please Him. He knows our hearts, and gives liberally to us who are willing, yielding servants.

> *"Pursue love, yet desire earnestly spiritual gifts."*
>
> 1 Corinthians 14:1

I don't know about you, but I think God might not want to give gifts to one who seeks their own glory. If we seek God with our whole hearts, then we will see His generous hand. Along with that hand comes blessings added to our lives:

> *"But seek first His kingdom and His righteousness, and all these things will be added to you."*
>
> Matthew 6:33

Remember that we are a whole Body. Each a member. It was never God's design for us to work alone, but to blend our gifts together for the benefit of the Church. Think of it as a weaving together of wonderful assets directly from heaven that we bring into one. For healing, exhortation, encouragement. If we find ourselves being jealous of others' gifts, then we must repent and sincerely ask for our own. God is both forgiving and giving.

We need to be faithful in order to spread the good news:

"The things which you have heard from me in the presence of many witnesses, entrust these to faithful men who will be able to teach others also."

2 Timothy 2:2

What are our benefits from receiving gifts?

When we receive gifts from the Holy Spirit, there are many benefits that follow. Not only are we giving to the Body blessings from above, we will also receive them. As we learn to use our gifts, we develop great skills that help us in our daily walks.

One is discernment to recognize God's will for our lives. To understand His ways in the spiritual realm. We'll have the power to overcome obstacles in our way by staying in His will. The Holy Spirit helps us to make good choices, spiritually mature decisions, and enables us to obtain solid focus. We'll learn to gain wisdom from above, not earthly wisdom from below.

There is nothing more rewarding or refreshing than when we reach out to others with God's gifts:

"In everything I showed you that by working hard in this manner you must help the weak and remember the words of the Lord Jesus, that He Himself said, 'It is more blessed to give than to receive.'"

Acts 20:35

And...

"Instruct them to do good, to be rich in good works, to be generous and ready to share, storing up for themselves the treasure of a good foundation for the future, so that they may take hold of that which is life indeed."

1 Timothy 6:18–19

In the following chapters, we will look closely at each of the service gifts. Let's keep our hearts open to hear what the Spirit will say to us concerning our gifts.

Time to Weigh In

Do you serve in your church or in a fellowship?

If so, what jobs or tasks do you believe you might employ within your service?

How long have you worked in a particular service?

Time to Grow

Write down some ways in which you might like to serve. Let's see if they match up with the descriptions of the service gifts in the following chapters.

Time to know

13

The Gift of Serving

"As each one has received a special gift, employ it in serving one another as good stewards of the manifold grace of God."

1 Peter 4:10

You might know why I chose this gift to start with. That you cannot lead without being a servant. To be of service to another is *diakonos*. It would be similar to an office of deacon. Although the gift of serving isn't for one particular position or purpose. It is multi-faceted, with many components that harmonize with all members throughout the entire church. Those with the gift of serving are able to identify and care for the many needs in the Body of Christ.

"For you were called to freedom, brethren; only do not turn your freedom into an opportunity for the flesh, but through love serve one another."

Galatians 5:13

I often think of service as having to do with those who have occupations as waiters, housekeepers, car mechanics, and such. But to be a servant in the Body of Christ comes with a great challenge. That is to stay humble, while working hard. But some believers with the gift of serving are overlooked. Overshadowed by the more admired gifts, like the gifts of healing, for instance.

The server must keep a good attitude with a motivational desire to demonstrate love by meeting practical needs. To do this, they should be willing to sacrifice their time and energy to complete their tasks. Tasks that they may not be so excited about doing. Like cleaning the bathrooms, or working in the nursery.

BUT ONE WITH THE TRUE GIFT OF SERVING WILL DO SO BY SIMPLY DOING WHATEVER IS NEEDED TO DO.

I truly admire the believer who has this gift. I appreciate and am thankful for their commitment to the Body. And so many of them have thankless jobs. A server's spiritual fulfillment comes when they've finished a task given to them. As we serve others, we are actually serving the Lord, who takes great pleasure in this.

> *"And whoever in the name of a disciple gives to one of these little ones even a cup of cold water to drink, truly I say to you, he shall not lose his reward."*
>
> Matthew 10:42

Jesus spoke often of the importance of serving. A leader is a servant and should be an example to the congregation as one. It is a very high calling. But we can't be a leader unless we serve:

> *"But the greatest among you shall be your servant."*
>
> Matthew 23:11

THE GIFT OF SERVING

The good character and strengths of a server most likely prevail over any of their weaknesses. It is truly a special calling. Most Christians that I've known who serve are special as well.

I knew a young man who used to sweat in the heat of the morning while stacking up chairs to bring them into a school auditorium for the Sunday service. And not only him, but the others who met there to also help. A large, heavy piano needed to be moved each week to the stage. Bulky sound equipment was hoisted up the stairs to the building. Long, wooden ramps were brought from someone's pick-up truck to get heavy objects onto the stage. Someone else brought the podium each week. Such hard work these men and women did. I always watched with respect for what they accomplished to bless the Body, while sacrificing their time and energy.

I know a woman who voluntarily searches the seats and floor of the church for trash or bulletins after each service. No one asks her to. She does it because it's her way to help serve the Body. Another woman would pick up the overflow of used, paper hand towels from the trash container in the ladies' room. Never without a cheerful smile on her face as she served. And all along, if no one else noticed, the Lord did:

> *"For God is not unjust so as to forget your work and the love which you have shown toward His name, in having ministered and in still ministering to the saints."*
>
> Hebrews 6:10

Servants are special people of God. They have His heart and wear it on their sleeves. Not to boast or to bring attention to themselves. But by doing the work of the Father in Jesus' name.

These volunteers are consistent and precise. They show up promptly and offer their time to do whatever tasks are at hand for the operation of the church, or an event. They don't grumble or complain, because after all, they are utilizing the very gift they were given. The gift of serving. A server will always be found with some of these characteristics:

Characteristics of a Server:

A Server Is:

1. A doer
2. Driven to serve by love
3. Good at meeting practical needs
4. A volunteer
5. Readily available
6. First to raise their hand for a job request
7. Orderly
8. Full of grace
9. Responsible

Notable Strengths of a Server:

A Server:

1. Enjoys doing menial chores
2. Loves to bless others
3. Has humility
4. Works alone to get the job done

5. Doesn't complain about their job
6. Envisions the finished product
7. Enjoys an event more if serving for it
8. Expresses their love through their work

Possible Challenges for a Server:

Servers Might:

1. Lose sight of spiritual priorities
2. Face temptation to become over-committed
3. Get frustrated with time limitations
4. Tend to overwork themselves
5. At times be demanding of others
6. Strive to be perfectionists

The gift of serving is usually physical work to serve the Body. Let's look at a few examples, and while we do, please bring along your own ideas to be added to the list:

- Pass out bulletins at the beginning of church
- Set up tables and chairs for church events
- Set up music equipment
- Seat people for the service
- Collect the offering
- Prepare communion
- Serve communion
- Paint the building
- Clean the church bathrooms
- Sweep the front steps of the church
- Mop the floors

- Clean the windows
- Work in the nursery
- Work the shuttle
- Organize the parking
- Direct traffic
- Plant flowers on the church property
- Drive a widow to a doctor's appointment

These are just some of the ways in which to physically serve the Church and the members. Thank you for adding to the list. And if you serve, I thank you for that too. And God thanks you:

> *"Give, and it will be given to you. They will pour into your lap a good measure—pressed down, shaken together, and running over. For by your standard of measure it will be measured to you in return."*
>
> Luke 6:38

Time to Weigh In

If you've served before, do you believe that your tasks were appointed within your gifting?

Have your serving positions been enjoyable for you or a burden to you?

Do you believe that you simply jump in to help now and then without realizing that you might have a particular gift in which to serve in?

Time to Grow

Are you aware, that as we serve, that we are serving the Lord?

Think of how others in your life serve with joy. Would you be able to match that joy?

Go above that?

14

The Gift of Leadership

"An overseer [leader] must be above reproach, the husband of one wife, temperate, prudent, respectable, hospitable, able to teach, not addicted to wine or pugnacious, but gentle, peaceable, free from the love of money. He must be one who manages his own household well, keeping his children under control with all dignity (but if a man does not know how to manage his own household, how will he take care of the church of God?), and not a new convert, so that he will not become conceited and fall into the condemnation incurred by the devil. And he must have a good reputation with those outside the church, so that he will not fall into reproach and the snare of the devil."

1 Timothy 3:2–7

This Scripture displays quite a standard for leaders to live up to. But one that is necessary for a leader to follow in order to qualify for such a responsible position in the Church. So many of us long to be a leader, but forget that a leader is also a teacher who incurs stricter judgment. The reason for this is because of the enormous responsibilities that come along with this title. It can be quite demanding and overwhelming, as a matter of fact. But the call comes with great honors and rewards as well.

Leader in the Greek is *hodēgos;* a guide. One who directs. A leader should have training and the ability to discern God's purpose for a body of believers. They need to be equipped to communicate, set goals, and motivate others to get involved in the church with their gifts.

It's very important for a leader to delegate tasks as well. They can easily get burned out from the work set before them if they don't. It truly helps if the leader is not one who wants to control everything, but will allow the blessings of service to fall on others as well. A leader is one person, and the body is many.

If the Christian seeking a role in leadership has done a good job with smaller tasks, then they may find favor with God and other believers to move onto bigger ones. This is why we should never turn away a small task:

"He who is faithful in a very little thing is faithful also in much."
Luke 16:10a

The role of leadership comes with great demands. The person seeking it should spend a good amount of time in the Word and in prayer. It's always beneficial to seek for counsel as well, asking for guidance as they do. To confirm the calling. We are not to work in this position in our own strength. A leader depends on the strength of the Lord for help to do his duty:

"I can do all things through Him who strengthens me."
Philippians 4:13

Let's look deeper into some other responsibilities that a leader undertakes and implements:

Teacher of God's Word

"Preach the word; be ready in season and out of season; reprove, rebuke, exhort, with great patience and instruction."
                                                2 Timothy 4:2–3

God's Word is alive and vitally important for the growth and well-being of the church. Leaders must have good teaching skills and must be teachable also. I can attest to the importance of this. I've been a leader to women for many years now and have learned the importance of remaining teachable. There is always a lot to learn, and a leader should always be open to learning more. And to never think they know it all.

To teach good, solid doctrine is an enormous undertaking. A leader must be grounded in the knowledge of the Word. It helps to have discernment in the Spirit to do so. To have wisdom from the Holy Spirit while reading the Word is a great advantage. The Holy Spirit teaches us all things and even what to say:

"For the Holy Spirit will teach you in that very hour what you ought to say."
                                                Luke 12:12

Do you see how the last two Scriptures above go together hand-in-hand? If we study the Word and allow the Holy Spirit to teach us, we will find it easy to deliver the doctrine correctly and set wrong to right:

"Remember those who led you, who spoke the word of God to you; and considering the result of their conduct, imitate their faith."
Hebrews 13:7

Leaders have charge over their flocks, which is the translation of *to stand before*, from the Greek word, *prohistemi*. A solidly based teacher will never abuse their authority to take advantage of others, or to pursue personal gain. This is why accountability is so important for leaders.

Accountable

There is a great deal of expectation from the church concerning the leader's own walk, which should be in good standing. Have you ever suspected that people were looking at you under a magnifying glass? To see if you make any mistakes? Or to prove to themselves that you aren't perfect? A sinner like themselves? If so, you can imagine what a hard position this is to be in. Even with my small little flock of women that I teach, comes a biblical standard of living that I need to follow. To live and behave like. To be a teacher, we must know we will be subject to judgment:

"Let not many of you become teachers, my brethren, knowing that as such we will incur a stricter judgment."
James 3:1

Does this mean that we should refrain from teaching altogether? Absolutely not. Who would teach if we're all afraid of being judged. God knows our shortcomings. We need to trust His judgments are true and fair. He is a just God and knows our frames, that we are weak. Let's glance at this:

"For we all stumble in many ways."

James 3:2

God knows our weaknesses and our sins. We can back away from serving the church, but that would be a mistake for all.

**NONE OF US ARE PERFECT TO TEACH,
SO LET'S TEACH WHILE WE'RE BEING PERFECTED.**

The best way to be accountable is to have one or two accountability partners. Those that you can comfortably confess your sins to, and glean godly advice from. We can look to them as well for encouragement to continue to sharpen our skills to serve.

"Therefore, confess your sins to one another."

James 5:16a

For myself, I have a few women that I'm accountable to. Women who live godly lives, who know the Word, who have the knowledge to counsel well, and who bring forth fruit in their own lives. I appreciate these dear friends, and thank God for them.

Exhorter and Encourager

A leader has the God-given ability to constructively motivate through exhortation and encouragement. Exhortation is a gift on its own. Hopefully, our leaders have that gift as well. To come alongside broken hearts and those in emotional, mental, and physical pain with timely words, consolation, and counsel. A leader might challenge one's faith by putting God's Word and ways in front of them. To test their faith and walk.

> *"And after the reading of the Law and the Prophets, the synagogue officials sent to them, saying, 'Brethren, if you have any word of exhortation, say it.'"*
>
> Acts 13:15

Christians need a lot of encouragement to carry on within the chaos of our world. Especially from their leaders. Look at it like this: A leader needs good parenting skills to lead their flock (their children) into spiritual maturity in Christ.

> *"That their hearts may be encouraged, being knit together in love and attaining to all wealth that comes from the full assurance of understanding, resulting in a true knowledge of God's mystery, that is Christ himself in whom are hidden all the treasures of wisdom and knowledge."*
>
> Colossians 2:2–3

Good Communicator, Counselor, and Listener

> *"This you know, my beloved brethren. But everyone must be quick to hear, slow to speak and slow to anger; for the anger of man does not achieve the righteousness of God."*
>
> James 1:19–20

How many times have you heard a complaint from a friend that their teacher (pastor) doesn't listen to them? Have you ever known teachers who love to hear themselves talk? That might sound a little harsh—but many people who teach fall into that category. And in the end, no one listens to them.

If you have many friends, I'll bet that you are a good listener. Everyone wants to be heard. It makes us seem loved. Important. It gives us confirmation that we are worthy of life and its blessings. It's key for anyone in ministry to speak well and to listen even better. Even if the person doesn't listen back. This is a leader's gift. Their claim to the position they've been deposited in. A leader is a good communicator and a good listener. It simply has to go both ways.

The congregation respects and looks up to its leader. But if that leader delivers monologues and never lets another get a word in—it's possible that they've missed their calling. Their motive to lead might not have been pure in the matter.

A qualified leader will be interested in listening to one of Christ's followers. To find out more about them, and to help serve them better. A mature leader will also glean any wisdom they can by listening. They have this ability, which is what led them to lead in the first place.

In church once, I was greatly disappointed when I ventured to share something so dear to me with my Bible teacher. The entire time I spoke, his eyes were taking in the busy room around us. He didn't hear a word I said. Someone then came and interrupted our conversation (which seemed rather dissatisfying at best). It didn't matter since my teacher wasn't interested anyway. I lost hope that I could come to him for counsel.

The truth is that every person matters. Every person should be made to believe that they are important to God and to us, as leaders. We all look up to our teachers, pastors, and leaders with godly reverence. But when we don't think that they care about us, we are sorely disappointed. Remember, they are human. The good news is that God listens. But for us, let's remember this:

"Let your speech always be with grace, as though seasoned with salt, so that you will know how you should respond to each person."
Colossians 4:6

Characteristics of a Leader:

A Leader Is:

1. A servant
2. A person with integrity
3. Truthful and honest
4. Patient with all
5. Zealous to teach
6. A good counselor
7. Without guile
8. Organized and methodical
9. Gifted to distinguish spirits
10. Good at handling criticism
11. Focused
12. Punctual
13. Equipped to minister at all times

Notable Strengths of a Leader:

A Leader:

1. Is ready and eager to teach the gospel
2. Can bring order to a disruptive meeting
3. Sees things through the eyes of God
4. Has good marriage counseling methods
5. Is a good listener
6. Has the ability to delegate
7. Loves unconditionally
8. Disciples their flock

Possible Challenges for a Leader:

A Leader Might:

1. Become burned out
2. Be affected by criticism
3. Become tempted with sin
4. Become dull of hearing
5. Become cold hearted
6. Get their eyes fixed on financial gain
7. Become arrogant and take glory for themselves
8. Become discouraged
9. Be a showman
10. Act with pride
11. Teach incorrect doctrine
12. Have favorites within the congregation

Some Tasks, Jobs, and Commitments of a Leader:

- Make decisions
- Schedule activities
- Budget time
- Delegate responsibility
- Motivate
- Put others before themselves
- Study and grow in knowledge
- Keep their own household in good order
- Organize meetings
- Be on the church board
- Oversee the church budget

Some Very Important Qualities Would Be:

- To know well and use correct doctrine
- To be loyal with tithing
- To be organized and prompt
- To display good fruit in their lifestyle
- To treat everyone fairly

Leaders are to be respected and loved by their followers. We need more leaders who have and practice all of the qualifications for this office. I encourage you to pray to become a leader if it is the will of God for your life. And if it is, His Spirit will appoint you to leadership. He will open the doors and guide you.

Time to Weigh In

Have you ever thought of yourself as a leader?

Were you a leader as a child?

What qualities do you have that would line up nicely with leadership?

Do you believe that the brethren would follow you as their leader?

Would you put those follower's best interest before yours?

Devotion is key in leadership. Have you a fickle or faithful heart toward others?

Time to Grow

If you've been given this gift, how, when, and what venue can you see yourself leading?

Has God given you direction in which to go forward with this gift?

Are you aware of the vast responsibilities that come along with this office?

If so, please take time to list some of them below:

15

The Gift of Exhortation

"Holding fast the faithful word which is in accordance with the teaching, so that he will be able both to exhort in sound doctrine and to refute those who contradict."

Titus 1:9

This Scripture was directed at leaders in the early Church, but still holds fast today. Elders and leaders were not to be self-willed, but self-controlled. This would guarantee that the exhortation was coming from God, not from themselves. To keep ourselves in submission to and under the influence of the Holy Spirit, and not to our flesh, keeps the pathway to discerning God's will for a situation clear. Here is a good verse to remind us the significance of self-control:

"For the overseer must be above reproach as God's steward, not self-willed, not quick tempered, not addicted to wine, not pugnacious, not found of sordid gain, but hospitable, loving what is good, sensible, just, devout, self-controlled."

Titus 1:7–8

And one as a metaphor:

"Like a city that is broken into and without walls is a man who has no control over his spirit."
Proverbs 25:28

I don't think any of us would appreciate a word from someone who had no self-control. Without godly control over ourselves, our gifts will become useless. Exhortation in the Greek is *paraklēsis;* to both build-up and correct the body of believers. This gift gives the ability to motivate others by providing timely, appropriate words of encouragement and counsel. Upon hearing a word of exhortation, the believer is challenged to put it to the test, knowing it came from God's throne room.

"Let the words of my mouth and the meditation of my heart be acceptable in Your sight, O LORD, my rock and my Redeemer."
Psalms 19:14

Have you witnessed someone in your church who always has a good word for someone? One who delights in blessing others with God's acknowledgments? There should be at least one, if not many members who have this gift. God, Himself, is the great Encourager of all. He exhorts us daily with His Word.

A woman, that I grew to admire, came to church always with a smile on her face. She would hug everyone and give many a lovely exhortation. But they weren't always what one might want to hear. Now and then she would speak forth some instruction to encourage them. The challenge proved a bit much for some. Yet, for others, a great blessing. Some were put off when she spoke of the blessings that come with tithing. Or when she exhorted a member to become involved in a certain ministry. But regardless of how they reacted, her interaction with them began and ended with a warm smile and hug. She'd walk away knowing that she did her job. And until the next time she'd be moved to come along to remind them with love, she had peace. She did her work for the Lord, not to please people.

It's important to have the right timing to present a word of exhortation to another. The timing should be God's, not ours. We need to watch and listen. Even a good word will seem useless if it is spoken to a heavy heart:

"Like one who takes off a garment on a cold day, or like vinegar on soda, is he who sings songs to a troubled heart."

Proverbs 25:20

But when the timing is right:

"Anxiety in a man's heart weighs it down, but a good word makes it glad."

Proverbs 12:25

When you have the gift of exhortation, you will receive many blessings, and also a few disappointed faces. I was born again in 1980. A time of jubilee for believers. A type of revival took place, and we were all excited to do great wonders for God. In the particular fellowship that I was involved in, we heard nothing but grandeur. All positive words twittered throughout the pews and in the courtyard. A negative word was never spoken.

At some point I wondered if anyone there had any trials in their lives. Were we all going to go through life as though we were already in heaven, now that we'd come to the Lord? I didn't really get it all until I had quite a trial myself that opened my eyes to a realistic walk with God. Then, I realized the importance of this gift. Every aspect of it.

WE ALL NEED A GOOD WORD AT A TIME WHEN THINGS GO FOUL IN OUR LIVES.
TO HAVE A HELPING OF HOPE ON OUR FULL PLATES.

Only a few short months after my commitment to God, my cousins asked me to fly up to northern California to share my life and new birth. I accepted the invitation with joy. Upon my arrival, my cousin offered me a glass of their well water. With great thirst, I drank it rapidly to quench the dryness in my throat. After consuming the entire glass, it left a strange taste in my mouth. The next day I awoke to find my face swollen. My eyes popped out like a frog. My vision seemed blurred.

How will anyone believe my testimony now? My vocation—a model and commercial actress. They won't believe that! I looked a fright. But a word of exhortation came through another cousin of mine who came that morning to hear me speak. She told me that God will go before me and speak through me. He will use the sudden change in my appearance for good. And her word of encouragement came with love.

She was right. I told everyone what had happened and it touched many. They were surprised that I stood in front of them to minister in my odd state of appearance. My message ended up being different from what I had planned. I shared of the many years in which I had to always look good. How my appearance determined the success of my career. I could see the reaction on the faces of the women. They could relate to my story.

God used a difficult circumstance to heighten my message that morning. He knew what this community needed, and used me as a type of sacrifice to do so. But it didn't stop there in that little church in Rocklin. The effect of the odd reaction lasted a long while. It actually ended my career as well. At the time, I was devastated. But long afterward, with many exhortations from believers, I ended up thanking God for the physical challenge.

My face eventually returned to normal. But I never forgot the lesson in that experience of transformation. The importance to build up the inner person and the ability to let go of something that was an enormous part of my life. And when my countenance returned, my soul blossomed.

The meaning of exhortation, as I mentioned before, is a calling to one's side. This is exactly what happened to me in Rocklin. Someone came alongside of me and encouraged and exhorted me to continue to speak at the church.

Jesus does the same with us daily. He uses believers to bless other believers. He brings someone to our aid in time of need. A Christian who has this valuable gift. The Holy Spirit speaks to us through other believers. We receive words of comfort and consolation through them from the Comforter, Himself.

We can easily lose heart in trials unless we have a good word from God. Our hearts can harden without the softening power of exhortation from another:

> *"But encourage [exhort] one another day after day, as long as it is still called "Today," so that none of you will be hardened by the deceitfulness of sin."*
>
> Hebrews 3:13

> *"These things speak and exhort and reprove with all authority. Let no one disregard you."*
>
> Titus 2:15

Those of us who have been generously given the gift of exhortation must never hold it back. If we obey God and bring forth an encouragement, He will minister to that person. We are the deliverer, He is the maker of our souls. God knows what we need to hear and when we need to hear it.

Can you imagine if God desired to give an exhortation to a believer through us and we held it in? What if that word could change that person's life? And out of our pride, laziness, or selfish nature, we withhold God's message? Thankfully, God is greater than that, and will seek another gifted person to deliver the message. But we miss out.

As we read more into God's remarkable ways, it becomes clearer to us how important it is to ask for and use the gifts of the Holy Spirit. And this gift will be beneficial wherever the gifted goes. In whatever they do.

Characteristics of an Exhorter:

An Exhorter Is:

1. A mature believer
2. Kind hearted
3. An encourager
4. Giving with their words
5. Honest and forthright
6. Edifying
7. Without gossip
8. Without jealousy
9. Without strife
10. Complementary
11. Giving with their time

Notable Strengths of an Exhorter:

An Exhorter:

1. Doesn't bring attention to oneself
2. Respects others' gifts and roles in the church
3. Doesn't covet what others have
4. Has kind speech
5. Has a generous heart
6. Seeks out individuals to build up

Possible Challenges for an Exhorter:

An Exhorter Might:

1. Speak out in the flesh instead of the Spirit
2. Not be correct at all times in their comments
3. Be tempted to flatter
4. Try and gain favor from their exhortation
5. Say things at an untimely manner

Various Ways an Exhorter Might be Used:

- Lead a group
- Teach classes of exhortation
- Teach Sunday school
- Minister unto the leadership and staff
- Have a one-on-one ministry

- Lead the choir
- Direct plays
- Encourage and teach others about the gifts
- Visit the sick and downcast

The gift of exhortation will bring many rewards to the gifted. It's a beautiful song to sad ears. A joyous rhythm to one frozen in fear. And a hopeful future for one with a sorrowful past. Pray now to seek this gift from the Spirit. I pray you will receive it.

Time to Weigh In

Do you think you have the ability to build up others?

Is it in your heart to see people succeed?

Have you exhorted others in a timely manner?

Time to Grow

Have you any jealousies toward any of the brethren that would stop you from exhorting them?

Think of your small group or fellowship friends. How would you exhort someone in that group?

If you've already exhorted people in your fellowship, do you believe that you were being led by the Holy Spirit?

How did it make you feel when you released an exhortation to another?

16

The Gift of Giving

"Each one must do just as he has purposed in his heart, not grudgingly or under compulsion, for God loves a cheerful giver."

2 Corinthians 9:7

Everyone in the family of Christ should give with a cheerful heart. If you have the gift of giving, you might automatically give with that attitude.

Believers with this gift need not be wealthy. But they have the ability to contribute material resources for the benefit of the growth of the church and others. And always to give glory to God. I think of the woman who gave all that she had without grumbling, but with a joyful heart:

"And He sat down opposite the treasury, and began observing how the people were putting money into the treasury; and many rich people were putting in large sums. A poor widow came and put in two small copper coins, which amount to a cent. Calling His disciples to Him, He said to them, 'Truly I say to you, this poor

widow put in more than all the contributors to the treasury; for they all put in out of their surplus, but she, out of her poverty, put in all she owned, all she had to live on."

Mark 12:41–44

God looks at our hearts. And when He saw this woman's, He was well pleased. Not only with her generosity but also the happiness that came along with it. By contrast to the wealthy Scribes, this widow worshipped God out of deep humility. She was genuinely devoted to giving.

Regardless of our income, it's not the amount in which we give that is important to God, but how much we retain. There is an obligation for us to pay directly to God out of what we've been given. We are commanded to do so.

WHETHER IF WE ARE WEALTHY OR POOR, THERE IS NO ONE EXEMPT FROM THE COMMANDMENT TO TITHE.

But there are some who go beyond that. They give their money, time, and skills to God and the Church. To give to God is to give to the poor, the needy, the weary. As Jesus had said, that if you give to one of these little ones, you've given to Him. He always has a heart for the poor, and desires for us to have his same heart toward the needy. We are to continue to give in His name, for His name's sake.

I personally find giving more rewarding when we do it in secret. When we do, our reward is great.

"But when you give to the poor, do not let your left hand know what your right hand is doing, so that your giving will be in secret; and your Father who sees what is done in secret will reward you."

Matthew 6:3–4

THE GIFT OF GIVING

To give in the Greek is *apodidōmi*. This means to present as an expression of honor and respect as in this Scripture:

"After coming into the house, they saw the Child with Mary His mother; and they fell to the ground and worshiped Him. Then, opening their treasures, they presented to Him gifts of gold, frankincense, and myrrh."

Matthew 2:11

People gave Jesus gifts out of great joy and celebration. We still give to Jesus as we give to others in need:

"The King will answer and say to them, 'Truly I say to you, to the extent that you did it to one of these brothers of Mine, even the least of them, you did it to Me.'"

Matthew 25:40

It is precious in the sight of the Lord to see His children behave like family. Who love one another and take care of one another. And with cheer. The Lord smiles upon us as He watches us become selfless. He also promises that we will be blessed by giving to others:

"And whoever in the name of a disciple gives to one of these little ones even a cup of cold water to drink, truly I say to you, he shall not lose his reward."

Matthew 10:42

I think we can grasp the idea that God loves a cheerful giver. So much so that He gives us the gift of giving. Charisma is a gift of grace, in which God blesses believers with endowments through the operation of the Holy Spirit. We are partakers of that grace. It is an honor to be used by God to give to others.

There are numerous people who love to give. I've witnessed people who have given a car to their pastor, or have paid for the down-payment toward their home. There have been fellow worshippers whom I've seen give their entire paycheck so that another could pay their rent.

BUT THERE ARE OTHER WAYS TO GIVE THAN MONETARILY. ONE IS GIVING OF TIME.

You might babysit a family's children so that the parents can have a date night. Or, you might wash someone's car. Time is valuable. And if you share it to serve another, you are giving. If you take off time and pay for a day to help another, in a round-about-way, you are giving them monetarily. But the joy in that giving comes from God.

> *"And God is able to make all grace abound to you, so that always having all sufficiency in everything, you may have an abundance for every good deed."*
>
> 2 Corinthians 9:8

I always loved to give, and even more so after I came to the Lord. I have blessed others out of my poverty and out of my abundance. I've had little, and I've had a lot. But I never went without food, clothing, or shelter because our God is faithful. I've learned to be content in all things. I think of this Scripture:

> *"At this present time your abundance being a supply for their need, so that their abundance also may become a supply for your need, that there may be equality; as it is written, 'HE WHO gathered MUCH DID NOT HAVE TOO MUCH, AND HE WHO gathered LITTLE HAD NO LACK.'"*
>
> 2 Corinthians 8:14–15

THE GIFT OF GIVING

I knew that I had a gift of giving even as a young child when my mother and my two sisters and I walked to town. On the side of the street, near the curb, I spotted a twenty-dollar-bill. I quickly picked it up and couldn't wait to give it to my mother, who desperately needed new lingerie. Although this happened a long time ago, I remember every detail of that day. When in bed that night, I replayed the moment over and over again.

This love of giving never went away, and only enhanced once my walk with Jesus began. I've seen others who share my sentiments in giving. One time some friends couldn't pay their rent. They prayed and waited for some money that was to be delivered to them in the mail. But on the day their rent was due, it hadn't arrived yet.

A knock was heard on their door, as the couple ventured to see who came to visit. A stranger to them presented a bright smile and an envelope, then raced off. The man and wife jetted over to their sofa to open it. Inside was cash. It added up to the amount of their rent. They both began to tear-up as they thanked God for the generous soul who sent them the gift.

They've shared this story many times over the years. But not only were they grateful for themselves for this rescue, they in-turn gave the money they'd been awaiting to some neighbors that were in need. Let's look at this promise:

"He who gives to the poor will never want."
                                        Proverbs 28:27a

This Scripture is so true. I have always given, and God has always given to me. The time that I couldn't pay my own rent, a check came the day it was due. I knew that it was God's hand, since I wasn't expecting any checks. For a year of low income, I only had a small salad and an apple each day. But He provided for what I needed, not necessarily what I wanted. Now and then someone would take me out to dinner, in which I knew to order protein each time. Even during that season of so little, I found myself sharing with others. God has given me a heart like His in giving. I sincerely thank Him for this gift.

To me, giving is more rewarding than receiving. If I can make someone smile, my heart rejoices. And you might be the same exact way. If you are, then you have the gift of giving. And I pray that you continue in that helpful gift throughout your lifetime here.

Characteristics of a Giver:

A Giver Is:

1. Unselfish
2. Kind-hearted
3. Generous
4. Compassionate
5. Timely
6. Cheerful

Notable Strengths of a Giver:

A Giver:

1. Gives and forgets that they gave
2. Wants no attention for their giving
3. Gets more joy from giving than receiving
4. Seeks out opportunities to be charitable

Possible Challenges for a Giver:

A Giver Might:

1. Give with a motive
2. Want recognition for their charity
3. Draw attention to themselves
4. Lack discernment on when and what to give

Ways for a Giver to Use the Gift of Giving:

- Organize a food ministry for the poor
- Create ways to give to the community
- Start a deacons' fund for the needy
- Orchestrate a mission trip to a poor country
- Get supplies to people in disaster-struck areas
- Distribute food to the community for holidays
- Start a fundraiser for a special cause
- Give their time and talents to the church

The act of giving should be used by every believer. The gift of giving is one that blesses all involved. I pray that we would each desire this beautiful gift. One that Jesus displayed so generously.

Time to Weigh In

Would you describe yourself as generous or not so?

Have you always been this way?

Does it give you great joy to give to others?

Time to Grow

When you see someone in need, do you have empathy for them, or do you think that it's somehow their problem?

You might already have this gift—but if not—are you willing to change anything within yourself in order to receive it?

Are you open to becoming a cheerful giver?

17

The Gift of Mercy

"Therefore, let us draw near with confidence to the throne of grace, so that we may receive mercy and find grace to help in time of need."

Hebrews 4:16

The Greek word, *eleos,* means an outward manifestation of one who is rich in mercy. A person gifted with mercy is one who has compassion upon people in need, hurting, or blinded by their own wrongdoings.

If you have the gift of mercy, you have the ability to engage in loving, compassionate acts with those who are suffering physically, emotionally, or mentally. You will never overlook people who are so often overlooked. You'll seek out the hurting in order to bring them consolation and hope. You do so with great kindness and selflessness.

Mother Teresa was one who without a doubt had the gift of mercy. What led her to give her all for others? The love of God in her heart and the gift of mercy, I'd guess. She exemplified and personified the love of Jesus to all she came into contact with. Her actions and motivations were unselfish and went beyond the expectations of so many.

Another woman reminds me of Mother Teresa. My maternal grandmother, Ida Golden. She couldn't travel, and wasn't known to millions. But she had the gift of mercy. She loved people unconditionally in their sin and misbehaving. Her gentle, soft ways would melt the hardness off of any heart. Ida didn't hold grudges. She forgave easily. And gave her all to so many.

The kind ways of my grandmother were abundant toward me. I'll always remember one time in particular when I was a teenager. She'd asked me to meet her at church one Sunday morning. I had been at a wedding reception the night before. I barely dragged myself to church, and made it up to the front row, where she always sat.

The leftover scents of alcohol and cigarette smoke clung to me. But that didn't move my sweet grandma. She threw her arms in the air with joy to see me and said, "Honey," with more love than you might imagine.

Ida had many gifts, but she truly utilized this gift with God's tender love. She is a profound reason why I eventually committed my life to the Lord. And because of her mercy for me, I was able to forgive myself for all of the many sins I had indulged over time. She was an example of God's own love to me. And forever, I am grateful to her.

This makes me think of the mercy seat. A symbol of God's amazing grace. His forgiveness. He made a way for His people to be forgiven of their sins through sacrifices. He incorporated that kind of love into this special gift. Mercy. And today the mercy of Jesus flows through us to others, as God has commanded us to love one another. Jesus told us to be merciful:

"Be merciful just as your Father is merciful."

Luke 6:36

THE GIFT OF MERCY

There are heart-warming ways to show mercy to others. We might take someone in need into our homes to live for a season. We might be led to give money, food, or supplies to the poor:

"He who despises his neighbor sins, but happy is he who is [merciful] to the poor."

Proverbs 14:21

The good Samaritan showed mercy to a stranger in need. He didn't worry about what others would say, or if he'd be accused of wrong doing. But he was driven by the love of God in his heart to help a man who had been beaten and left to die. Mercy flowed from his heart, and he saved a man's life.

To be Christ-like is an important part of the gift of mercy. We can courageously approach God in prayer about our own sins because we know that He is loving, kind, and forgiving. And full of mercy. Therefore, we can be the same to others, so that they will deem us approachable. It's my own personal belief that all believers should desire and seek for this gift.

Each of us are flawed from the past pains and trials of our lives. God enables us to grow in mercy to become healthy vessels for His glory. He even allows certain events to take place in order to move our hearts toward the needs of others.

AS GOD HAS GIVEN US MERCY, IT'S IMPORTANT FOR US TO SHOW THAT SAME MERCY TO OTHERS.

"I thank Christ Jesus our Lord, who has strengthened me, because He considered me faithful, putting me into service; even though I was formerly a blasphemer and a persecutor and a violent aggressor. And yet I was shown mercy, because I acted ignorantly in unbelief."

1 Timothy 1:12–13

There are many people in the world who are as Paul. He was a murderer of Christians. A great sinner. But God saw potential in that man. He didn't give up on Paul, as we mustn't give up on others. By showing people mercy and praying for them we can dramatically change their lives. They might become an important part in the Body. Just as Paul. Those who have great contrast in their conversions have the ability to draw many hearts toward God with their power-packed testimonies.

Years ago, I saw a newspaper photo of the young man who killed three of my friends. Love welled in my heart for him. I knew that it came from God. Mercy-driven tears rolled down my cheeks as I prayed for God to forgive him. I also prayed that this person would repent and come to know the Lord.

Many years later, I looked him up online to find that he accepted Jesus in prison. That he has a ministry there to other prisoners. Oh, the mercy of God! And to think that He appointed me to pray for him at a time such as that.

God's mercy is never ending. Let's ask for His mercy to settle upon our hearts for others in need. Those who long for the loving hand of God to show that He still loves them. And that He does so through you and me.

Characteristics of the Merciful:

One with Mercy Is:

1. Tender hearted
2. An excellent listener
3. Forgiving
4. Gracious
5. Full of God's love

6. Non-judgmental
7. Compassionate
8. Encouraging
9. Humble in nature

Notable Strengths of a Merciful Person:

A Merciful Person:

1. Doesn't display anger
2. Respects others
3. Fears God
4. Doesn't gossip

Possible Challenges for a Merciful Person:

A Merciful Person Might:

1. Have a difficult time discerning evil
2. Give generous advice to dead ears
3. Easily be taken advantage of
4. Be unable to say no

Some Ways One with Mercy Might Contribute:

- Start a class on forgiveness
- Reach out to those in need

- Find ways to get others involved
- Counsel people
- Show love to the unloved
- Bring peace among others
- Pour out compassion on the suffering and afflicted
- Pray to break strongholds in people's lives

We all admire those with mercy. All believers have a portion of mercy from God. But to seek the Holy Spirit for more, and to ask God for this gift, can bring us priceless years to behold.

Time to Weigh In

Have you always been forgiving?

How about with someone whom you've really been hurt by?

Do you find yourself tearing-up when you see someone in pain or in great need?

Time to Grow

If you were attending a meeting, and noticed someone alone in the room, would you make a move to introduce yourself and start up a conversation?

Are you willing to show mercy to those who don't deserve it?

Would you sacrifice your time for someone in great need?

18

The Gift of Teaching

"And God has appointed in the church, first apostles, second prophets, third teachers."

1 Corinthians: 12:28a–c

One who teaches gives instruction. The word in the Greek that depicts a teacher is *didaskalos*. One who is rendered teacher of what is good is called *kalodidaskalos*. To teach diligently, is *shānan*. Teachers of the truth in the churches. This gift comes with great responsibility. Not one to take lightly. Here's the reason why, as we also read in the leadership chapter:

"Let not many of you become teachers, my brethren, knowing that as such we shall incur a stricter judgment."

James 3:1

There are necessary reasons for this. In order to teach others properly, we first need to know our subject matter well. That starts with Jesus. Once we have a relationship and foundation in Him, we must read His Word well. Rightly dividing the Word of truth. Through our teaching, we must provide a straight path for the Body. To keep them in line with His Word and His ways. If we handle the word of truth in an accurate way, we'll be able to avoid useless debates. If we stay focused on the straight way ahead, we'll reach our goal of teaching well.

WE MUST TEACH NOT WHAT IS OF MAN, BUT WHAT IS OF THE HOLY SPIRIT!

As we do, let's keep in mind that the Holy Spirit is our ultimate Teacher:

> *"Now, we have received not the spirit of the world, but the Spirit who is from God, that we might know the things freely given to us by God, which things we also speak, not in words taught by human wisdom, but in those taught by the Spirit, combining spiritual thoughts with spiritual words."*
> 1 Corinthians 2:12–13

To teach well, we need to study and be approved. It's important that we take time to learn how to put a good lesson together. In a way that will keep the listeners' attention to the very end. Words that will stick in the believers' minds, that they can revisit time after time.

Once we've accomplished this, we can trust the Holy Spirit to give us divine unction to present the lesson well. So, preparation is important, only if we seek for and accept the Holy Spirit's anointing on us—and our lesson—to convey a powerful message. And He is faithful to do just that.

You can teach even if you're an ordinary person like me. After many years of my teaching the Bible to women, the revelation has been made clear to me, time and time again, that the Holy Spirit teaches and speaks through me. As I yield, that is. As long as we teach what is right and true (good doctrine) we can't go wrong. And remember, God looks upon us with favor as we make these bold steps to teach His flock that He's appointed to us. Even if we teach to only a few people, it's good to teach to the best of our ability. And we should never despise small beginnings. If we handle them well, God will give us larger opportunities. I can't get enough of this Scripture:

> *"He who is faithful in a very little thing is faithful also in much."*
> Luke 16:10

Characteristics of a Teacher:

A Teacher Is:

1. Studied and learned in the Word
2. A good speaker
3. Patient
4. Direct
5. Uncompromising about Scripture
6. Understandable
7. Anointed by God for teaching

Notable Strengths of a Teacher:

A Teacher:

1. Encourages through their teaching
2. Wants people to learn and prosper
3. Speaks clearly
4. Advices with knowledge

5. Doesn't boast in their knowledge
6. Judges fairly
7. Projects a clear picture of their message

Possible Challenges for a Teacher:

A Teacher Might:

1. Develop spiritual pride
2. Be tempted to teach with fleshly knowledge
3. Show favorites in their class
4. Boast in their knowledge
5. Give glory to themselves

Some Ways a Teacher Might Contribute:

- Offer their expertise of knowledge
- Teach the Word to groups in the church
- Give their time to teaching Sunday school
- Be an example of good teaching
- Create curriculum for church classes

Good teachers are hard to come by. Have you ever thought about teaching? If you have a desire to teach, please pray and ask if God has this valuable gift for you from the Holy Spirit.

Time to Weigh In

Have you taught before?

If so, did you teach adults, youth, or children?

Did you get enjoyment in teaching others?

Describe your experience, or multiple ones:

If you have taught, did you sense that people enjoyed your style of teaching?

Did you have a sense of reward afterward?

Time to Grow

If you've never taught, was there something that held you back?

Are you a shy person, or a sociable one?

Do you have a good grasp of the Word?

If not, would you be willing to study and learn more?

Have you ever been asked to teach?

If so, what was it for?

Were you comfortable teaching?

Have you any fear of not performing well in the area of teaching?

If true, please describe why you think this is:

If you have taught or even do so now, do you believe that you have been gifted by the Holy Spirit to teach?

If not, would you be willing to ask Him for that gift?

If yes, why—or if no, why?

19

The Gift of Ministering

"In pointing out these things to the brethren, you will be a good [minister] of Christ Jesus, constantly nourished on the words of faith and of the sound doctrine which you have been following."

1 Timothy 4:6

A minister in the Greek is *diakonos;* a servant, minister, attendant, deacon. He who ministers in the Greek is *leitourgos;* one who has priestly services. Above all, Jesus had this gift as the High Priest. Those of us who want to minister within the church will practice spiritual ministration. Some of us, I like to call, "Wait upon ministers." Those who look and wait for people who need ministry. Then approach them with gentleness and care.

In most cases, ministering is serving. If you have the gift of ministering, then you might have the gift of serving. They mingle together. It might be difficult to distinguish between the two.

I knew a man who sat in the back of the church named John. If he saw someone come in late, and cower in the back pews, he would minister to them at first chance. He could resonate with their personalities, having done this for years. He utilized the gift that He'd received from the Lord, using learned wisdom.

Another example of ministering would be to take care of one who is ill. To perhaps sing hymns and praises to them while they're recovering. Or read the Word to them.

For a season, my grandmother, Ida, took care of the ailing in her home. At one time she had five people living with her. They were all bedridden and couldn't walk. She took care of each one. She ministered to them as she fed them. Took care of their personal needs, and prayed over them continually. Another way in which to minister. And she did it with the love of Christ.

Was my grandmother gifted with ministering? Yes. I believe that this was one of her most appreciated gifts from God. She diligently performed duties to help other believers no matter the cost. And always with a smile on her face and a song in her heart.

AN ACT OF KINDNESS IS LIKE A COOL DRINK OF WATER TO A PARCHED SOUL.

When I was a baby believer, I met a man named Greg. He was a loving Christian who had great compassion for all in distress. I'll never forget one day at church when Greg stayed after the service and ministered to a hurting congregant for hours. And even though we had plans to go to lunch with him, he chose to stay to take care of this person. He always put others before himself. And this act of kindness, he displayed many other times as well. He had been given this gift. It seemed like he was just born that way. A true blessing to the church.

There is a plethora of ways to minister to another. If it's our gift, it comes easily. We'll always be attuned to a nearby sigh, or a need of someone. And that need will become paramount to any other, even our own. To minister in this manner reveals our love for Christ. If we give someone a cup of water, we give it unto the

Lord. As we attend to the poor, our hearts fill up with the love of Jesus, and we fulfill our duty to Him.

> *"For whoever gives you a cup of water to drink because of your name as followers of Christ, truly I say to you, he will not lose his reward."*
> Mark 9:41

Characteristics of a Minister:

A Minister Is:

1. Never self-serving
2. One that looks out for the good of others
3. Anointed to have eyes to see the lost and hurting
4. Never too busy for anyone
5. Selfless
6. Not prideful
7. A healing balm to the weary
8. An encourager

Notable Strengths of a Minister:

A Minister:

1. Makes time to minister when there is none
2. Prioritizes their schedules to be available
3. Always spots a hurting soul
4. Gets blessed as they're blessing others
5. Speaks into others' lives with wisdom

6. Cares about the privacy of one's life
7. Does what's right in the sight of the Lord

Possible Challenges for a Minister:

A Minister Might:

1. Become overwhelmed ministering over time
2. Easily be taken advantage of
3. Use their gift for opportunity
4. Be hurt by the one they minister to

Some Ways a Minister Might Contribute:

- Become a part of the prayer team
- Lead a Bible study or prayer group
- Visit the sick and comfort them
- Spend time helping the elderly
- Counsel the downtrodden
- Orchestrate a healing ministry

What a wonderful and useful gift this is! To be able to minister to others in the Holy Spirit. I believe that all believers should seek it. We need more ministering in our churches today than ever before, don't you think?

Time to Weigh In

Do you enjoy comforting others?

Have you ever been on a ministry team?

Can you count on your fingers how many people you've ministered to?

Or have there been so many that you can't count?

Time to Grow

If you see someone distraught, do you find it hard to refrain from approaching them to help?

If you have helped, did your ministering to them prove to give them comfort?

If you haven't ministered to someone, what do you think it is that holds you back?

Do you have a fear of getting close to others? Would this stop you from ministering to them?

20

The Gift of Apostleship

"Greet Andronicus and Junias, my kinsmen and my fellow prisoners, who are outstanding among the apostles, who also were in Christ before me."
Romans 16:7

Apostle in the Greek is *apostolos;* one sent forth. Apostle also means, "sending a mission." If one is sent out into the world, they are following Jesus' great commission. But we can also reach out to those who live next door to us. Those at work. We can go forth into our neighborhoods and touch those who have never heard the gospel. Those who have never been ministered to.

I walk around my neighborhood every day. I usually pray before I do, and ask God to guide me to anyone in need of salvation or prayer. Not long after I moved into my home in Santa Monica, CA, I prayed before every walk. But one day, before my usual walking time, God spoke to me. He asked me to go on my walk right then. Although it was early for me, and I'd preferred to go later, I obeyed His command.

As I ventured out, I walked north. Only after one block, I noticed a young man about the age of my sons. As I came closer to him, we both noticed the smell of gas coming from an old, deserted apartment complex. This brought us together and opened up a door of conversation. After we realized that there was no danger at hand, we went on with our walks side by side. We walked for two hours.

Matthew asked me all about God. He shared that he was brought up as a Christian, but really never experienced a close relationship with Jesus. Joy filled my heart that God had given me an opportunity to reach out to this sweet soul.

Apostleship? In a way, yes. Sometimes we get hung up on big titles. Let's look back at the description of apostleship once more: "One sent forth." As God sent me forth to minister to this man, the delicious fruit of salvation blossomed. The role of an apostle isn't beyond ordinary people like you and me. As we invite small beginnings into our lives, who knows what doors God will open. If we follow the Holy Spirit's leading, we will live like Jesus did. Paul followed the Lord's apostolic calling:

> *"Paul, a bond-servant of Christ Jesus, called as an apostle, set apart for the gospel of God, which He promised beforehand through His prophets in the holy Scriptures, concerning His Son, who was born of a descendant of David according to the flesh, who was declared the Son of God with power by the resurrection from the dead, according to the spirit of holiness, Jesus Christ our Lord, from whom we have received grace and apostleship to bring about the obedience of faith among all the Gentiles for His name's sake, in whom you also are the called of Jesus Christ."*
>
> Romans 1:1–6

By saying he was an apostle, Paul placed himself among the twelve apostles. He claimed authority from God for his work. The

THE GIFT OF APOSTLESHIP

purpose of his work was to persuade people to obey God's command to trust Jesus.

Others were also appointed to apostleship through Paul's example. Often, we forget that there were numerous apostles. Not just the twelve disciples of Jesus. Let's not forget Paul, Barnabas, Junias, and Andronicus.

The gift of apostleship is still given today. It's needed for the furthering and oversight of new churches. With this gift, one has the ability to begin or oversee Christian ministries with godly authority. Look at this with me:

"And God has appointed in the church, first apostles."
1 Corinthians 12:28a

Godly order comes into this line up. Apostles begin the development of a new church, then these other gifts come into play: Prophets, teachers, miracles, gifts of healing, helps, administrations, and various kinds of tongues.

Since Jesus' time was limited on earth, He used His apostles in order to testify to mankind concerning the gospel. His last words to them were a command:

"And He said to them, 'Go into the world and preach the gospel to all creation.'"

He gave us power, then He ascended:

"But you shall receive power when the Holy Spirit has come upon you; and you shall be My witnesses both in Jerusalem, and in all Judea and Samaria, and even to the remotest part of the earth. And after He had said these things, He was lifted up while they were looking on, and a cloud received Him out of their sight."
Acts 1:8–9

We too are to obey this command until the day He returns. We've become the Lord's servants to carry on the work that He started. This command should be taken seriously. That last instruction that Jesus left for us was a hugely important one. I will never forget the last words that my dear mother said to me before she departed for heaven. Likewise, I will never forget His.

Characteristics of an Apostle:

An Apostle Is:

1. Appointed by God
2. Ready to solve church problems
3. A lover of the Body at large
4. Orderly and organized
5. Able to teach, minister, and pray for others
6. An overseer of many facets of the church's growth
7. A visionary

Notable Strengths of an Apostle:

An Apostle:

1. Focuses on the tasks at hand
2. Sees things through to fruition
3. Has endurance
4. Has ears to hear God's instructions
5. Understands the importance of one-on-one ministry
6. Moves in signs and wonders

Possible Challenges for an Apostle:

An Apostle Might:

1. Lose sight of deadlines
2. Spend too much time away from family
3. Get their priorities out of godly order
4. Be puffed up because of their title

Things That Apostles Might Do:

- Find ways to grow the Church at large
- Build up the local church
- Travel to meet other believers in the world
- Unite people in Christ
- Go out into the world to preach, serve, and teach

You might be an apostle. Ask God to confirm this gift to you by the Holy Spirit. At this time in history, apostles are needed.

Time to Weigh In

Have you ever desired to start up a church whether in your own home, or in a building, or within a denomination?

Do you grasp the importance of witnessing and ministering one-on-one as well while using your spiritual gifts?

How invested have you been within the activities of your church and its growth?

Do you have the ability to build something from scratch?

To stay focused to the fruition of a project?

Is your heart filled with desire to save souls by reaching out?

Time to Grow

Would you consider opening up your home for a small Bible study?

Use your imagination: Think of a way that you could eventually contribute to the growth of the Church at large. What does that look like to you?

21

The Gift of Helps

"Now I urge you, brethren (you know the household of Stephanas, that they were the first fruits of Achaia, and that they have devoted themselves for the ministry to the saints), that you also be in subjection to such men and to everyone who helps in the work and labors."
1 Corinthians 16:15–16

The gift of helps in Greek is *antilēmpsis,* which means to take hold of and change. As to support a person. Rendering assistance to the weak and needy. Giving grace and timely help. To assist people with chores and tasks. In any case, it is mostly regarded as a physical help. But not all helps require physical strength.

The gift of helps gives the gifted the ability to enhance the effectiveness of the ministry of other members of the Body. It seems distinct from the gift of service. The gift is more person-oriented in some ways, yet still can be physically demanding. Doing unto others what they can't do for themselves.

My Grandmother, Ida, had this gift among many others. This one stood out the most, though. She was a charter member of the

Assembly of God Church in Covina, California, as well as one of the founders. Devoted in every way.

From the very beginning, Ida was a hands-on volunteer. Whatever task needed doing, she was the first in line to take it on. From sweeping the floors, to decorating the hall for a wedding reception, her eager hands reached out. She cooked and washed dishes in the church kitchen. And I mean, huge pots and pans. She'd grab the closest apron and stand in the same position at the farmer's-style sink for hours. At times, even into the early hours of the morning.

Having polio while growing up left her body crooked. She lived with constant pain, but you'd never guess it. And this was her way of giving and helping, since she couldn't give much monetarily. Her work was not in vain. God saw her every effort to serve Him and the Church.

I remember after a long night of her cleaning up at church, she took my hand and walked me across the alley to put me to bed in her tiny house. After locking me in, she'd march back to that kitchen until everything sparkled. A few hours later, I'd hear her slip into her bed with groaning. Not begrudging her duties, but addressing her bodily pain.

The next day, she'd start up again. Cleaned her own house first, then shot across the alley to the back door of the church to pray for the needy. And always with a loving, smile.

I've witnessed many beautiful sisters and brothers in the Lord throughout the years work hard like my beloved Ida did. God must give them extra portions of grace to handle the physical and emotional demands of various helps. After all, God loves a cheerful helper.

The gift of helps is very rewarding. To know that you've served the Body in such a tiring, yet tireless way can make one's heart warm within. Let's read ahead to see if we fit into this way of serving. A gift with many rewards.

Characteristics of a Helper:

A Helper Is:

1. Humble hearted
2. Available to help in a myriad of ways
3. Generous about giving of time
4. Unselfish

Notable Strengths of a Helper:

A Helper:

1. Starts helping without being asked
2. Needs no recognition for their help
3. Sacrifices their own time to serve
4. Truly loves to help others
5. Has no particular motive to give

Possible Challenges for a Helper:

Helpers Might:

1. Find it hard to say no
2. Get in the way of others because of their zeal to help
3. Be taken advantage of
4. Have to try hard to minimize self-praise

Examples of Tasks a Helper Might Do:

- Stay up all night to help a sick widow
- Pack goods to take to a halfway house
- Set up chairs and tables for church events
- Clean dishes after an event
- Help in the nursery
- Babysit for families with low income
- Assist the special needs members
- Decorate for holiday or special events
- Serve communion
- Comfort those grieving
- Help out with field trips

There is a high demand for helpers in churches. I pray that God will raise more of His people up to be helpers for His kingdom. The Holy Spirit will anoint them for the works ahead.

Time to Weigh In

Do you enjoy working alone, or with a group, or both?

Are you physically in shape in order to lift and move heavy objects? And/or are you equipped with emotional and spiritual strengths to help others?

Do you jump right in to help when someone needs assistance?

Time to Grow

Would you be willing to sign up for helps at your church with determination and desire to do your job well?

If so, list some tasks in which you imagine would come under the gift of Helps:

22

The Gift of Administration

"And God has appointed in the church, first apostles, second prophets, third teachers, then miracles, then gifts of healings, helps, administrations, various kinds of tongues."

1 Corinthians 12:28

Administration or ministration is *diakonia* in the Greek. Meaning the office and works of helps. Domestic duties, religious and spiritual duties, and administration work in a local church. The service of believers for the operation of the church.

People with administrative gifts support apostolic ministry, and are usually gifted to stay put and maintain that ministry after an apostle establishes it.

A person with this helpful gift has the ability and knowledge to build up and expand the ministry of other members in the church. It is simply a gift of service. They would be able to skillfully manage the affairs of the church and to implement and execute plans for its furthering. To help guide and direct toward fulfilling goals by managing with leadership skills as given and led by the Holy Spirit.

Karla, a mother of three, offered her extra time to do the accounting at her church while her children attended school. Not only did this help with the church's budget, but also allowed more time for the pastor and his wife to counsel and minister to its members. Karla never missed a carpool or one of her children's extra curriculum activities during the tenure of her voluntary work. It was apparent to the church that Karla had the gift of administration.

Ralph, a full-time construction engineer, drafted blueprints for the buildings that he built. He gave up his evenings to work on a plan for the expansion of his church's sanctuary. No one else in the congregation shared similar talents as Ralph's—whose long hours of hard work for the Body did not go without notice and appreciation. His efforts benefited all.

A church with good administration is able to function in an organized fashion, which can be fruitful in many ways.

"So that you may walk in a manner worthy of the Lord, to please Him in all respects, bearing fruit in every good work and increasing in the knowledge of God."

Colossians 1:10

Congregants who rise up to serve in this gift are a true blessing to the pastor of their church, as well as the members. Pastors must delegate, so that they don't become weary in doing good. Others need to come alongside of them, in order to help execute some of the voluminous responsibilities of running a church. If they don't, the result could be that they end up with an unorganized church and a tired-out leader. We should all use our gifts that God has appointed to us regardless of what they are, without coveting the gifts of other believers.

THE GIFT OF ADMINISTRATION

EACH GIFT HAS A PURPOSE IN THE CHURCH, AND IS THE VERY THING THAT KEEPS IT AFLOAT.

Characteristics of an Administrator:

An Administrator Is:

1. Loyal to their church
2. Responsible and accurate in a timely fashion
3. Confidential and trustworthy
4. Able to handle tasks with patience
5. Accountable in all ways
6. Functional without being easily distracted
7. Full of wisdom from God

Notable Strengths of an Administrator:

An Administrator:

1. Has organizational skills
2. Has pure motives within their work
3. Solves problems with ease
4. Gets advice and counsel from others
5. Works hard to fruition
6. Is able to communicate problems with grace
7. Has good business knowledge
8. Finishes their work to fruition
9. Works well in almost any environment

Possible Challenges for an Administrator:

An Administrator Might:

1. Be tempted to share private information
2. Want praise for their intellect
3. Desire to control others
4. Finish a job prematurely

Some Various Ways to Serve Under the Guidance of This Gift:

- Apply both spiritual and physical helps
- Implement plans for future growth
- Office work
- Keep books, budget
- Offer financial input and advice
- Hire and overlook staff and volunteers
- Book events
- Orchestrate group Bible studies
- Organize strategic planning committees

Good things come from hard work. As we diligently bind our efforts together to create a good foundation to learn and grow, we will accomplish much for our God and His Church. If this is your gift, know that you are truly appreciated for all you do.

Time to Weigh In

Do you have organizing skills that you've used in the past?

Are you punctual and functional?

Do you have the ability to be precise and deliver detailed work?

Time to Grow

Are you willing to sign up on the clipboard that circulates around the group meeting for this type of work?

Does your heart warm up when opportunity to serve presents itself?

Is there administrative experience in your past?

23

The Gift of Evangelism

"Preach the word; be ready in season and out of season; reprove, rebuke, exhort, with great patience and instruction."

2 Timothy 4:2

The Greek word for evangelist is *euangelistēs,* which means "a messenger of good." A preacher of the gospel not necessarily holding the office of a pastor. One who proclaims glad tidings. Missionaries are evangelists. But the gift itself may be given to one who simply loves to share the Bible and the message of salvation. It doesn't require someone to travel, but to evangelize wherever they are.

In the early days of my walk with Christ, an elder in the church I was attending laid hands on me and prophesied that I'd become an evangelist. Since I was young in the Lord, without much knowledge of the Word of God yet, I questioned this man's words. I didn't have a desire to travel afar, but loved to share about my new life in the Lord with all I'd come into contact.

Later on, as I became more mature, the calling seemed more clearer to me. I discovered that I could do the work of an evangelist within my ministry, as it explains here:

"But you, be sober in all things, endure hardship, do the work of an evangelist, fulfill your ministry."
2 Timothy 4:5

The Lord has been very generous and gracious to me. The Holy Spirit gifted me with several gifts. At first I was a little confused. What gift was what? What duties did each gift come with? It took time to identify each one and to discover more about them as I studied the Word and learned through my own experiences. I remain grateful each day to be used with my gifts.

An evangelist has one goal. To share the gospel with others. The news of salvation. A pastor has many duties and goals. So do leaders. But you can actually have this gift by itself and fulfill its calling in your life.

Characteristics of an Evangelist:

An Evangelist Is:

1. Gifted with a variety of the gifts
2. Caring and compassionate
3. A good communicator
4. Confident in their calling
5. Able to teach with boldness and conviction
6. A steadfast believer
7. Available at all times to share their own stories
8. Patient concerning others

Notable Strengths of an Evangelist:

An Evangelist:

1. Has a good sense of timing
2. Is able to discern
3. Is ready at each turn to share the gospel
4. Is well grounded in the Word
5. Has a heart to see all saved
6. Has stable and sound emotions

Possible Challenges for an Evangelist:

An Evangelist Might:

1. Become prideful
2. Step out in the flesh
3. Speak up when they shouldn't
4. Cast their pearls before swine
5. Take advantage of their high position

Ways in Which to Serve as an Evangelist:

- Organize street evangelism events
- Speak at other churches
- Have a one-on-one ministry
- Teach at Bible studies
- Bring many to Christ

- Write books to share of Christ
- Minister to politicians and leaders
- Travel to the ends of the earth to save souls

In many ways, we are all evangelists. But if you have the gift of evangelism, you have a drive and hunger in you to save souls like none other. Go with this gift, my friend, and may the Lord use you in magnificent ways to further His kingdom!

Time to Weigh In

Are you the type of person that wants to save the world, or to be content with saving a few?

Do you have the heart of God that drives you to cry out for souls?

Are you willing to travel to far places in order to save those who have never heard the gospel?

Time to Grow

Have you ever shared the gospel with another?

With a group or large crowd?

If so, were you confident and comfortable doing so?

Do you see yourself sharing the gospel in various ways in your life?

24

The Gift of a Pastor

"Shepherd the flock of God among you, exercising oversight not under compulsion, but voluntarily, according to the will of God; and not for sordid gain, but with eagerness."

1 Peter 5:2

The Greek word, *poimēn*, means a shepherd. One who tends herds or flocks. It is used metaphorically of Christian pastors. Pastors are not only to feed the flock as a shepherd does, but they also are to teach and guide them. They are to watch over them and make sure that they live well and finish well.

The gift of a pastor gives the ability to one who is tender hearted, willing to supervise and minister in all ways for his flock of believers. The flock that God has trusted them with.

This gift comes with a vastly heavy load of responsibilities. If the tasks are not handled well in timely manners, and with wisdom from God, pastors might get easily wearied. This could lead to them having to take long breaks away from their congregants to be refreshed and to restore their souls.

Peter, a disciple of Jesus, was commanded by the Lord, Himself, to shepherd His sheep. To attend to His flocks, as described in John 21. When Jesus announced the building of His Church, he gave the keys to the kingdom of heaven to him. Jesus called Peter His rock, on which the Church would be built:

> *"I also say to you that you are Peter, and upon this rock I will build My church; and the gates of Hades shall not overpower it."*
> Matthew 16:18

To be gifted with the office of pastor is of tremendous help to one who chooses this vocation. But not all pastors have this gift, and could find this office to be a stiff challenge at best. I knew a pastor who truly didn't like people that much. He even proclaimed this from the pulpit. But because he had charisma and a beautiful singing voice, he drew people to his church.

Later, though, this same man ran out of steam. He grew tired and weary of all the hard work at hand. His good judgments ceased. His mind became foggy. His body, weak. His own family became dysfunctional. And finally, he lost his flock.

This isn't the case for everyone. But I will say again, that it's far better to have the gift of the office of pastor to be one.

There is a warning to shepherds (pastors) in Jeremiah:

> *"My people have become lost sheep; Their shepherds have led them astray."*
> Jeremiah 50:6a–b

Here is an exhortation for gifted pastors:

> *"Be on guard for yourselves and all your flock, among which the Holy Spirit has made you overseers."*
> Acts 20:28a

A person gifted as a pastor is equipped for the job. They're full of faith that helps in their vocation. They are gifted to teach and minister without wearing out. That is if they stay within the boundaries of their gift and learn how to delegate well. If they choose solid Christians to work with them, they will fare well.

Characteristics of a Pastor:

A Pastor Is:

1. Loyal to his flock
2. A peacemaker
3. A person of their word
4. A good teacher of the Bible
5. Accountable to elders and deacons
6. A good leader
7. A good listener
8. A good counselor
9. Unwavering in their faith

Notable Strengths of a Pastor:

A Pastor:

1. Can control their flesh
2. Can rebuke, reproof, encourage, and edify
3. Lines up their thoughts with the Word
4. Benefits from the gift of discernment
5. Has the ability to love unconditionally

Possible Challenges for a Pastor:

A Pastor Might:

1. Be tempted to sin
2. Become prideful
3. Have a tendency to control
4. Develop favorites within the congregation
5. Neglect a spouse and/or family
6. Not delegate his work enough
7. Get burned out easily

Duties and Tasks of a Pastor:

- Teach the flock
- Study hard to implement new, fresh messages
- Be an example to the church
- Counsel members of the congregation
- Oversee the staff in a spiritual sense
- Keep harmony among the members
- Lead and guide in truth

I respect pastors and all that they do for us. Each one has their own style, their own methods of teaching. They all deserve our reverence for them if indeed they are anointed by the Holy Spirit. If you have a desire to pastor a church, I agree with you in prayer that our Lord will gift you. And may He bless you and your flock.

Time to Weigh In

Have you ever thought about being a pastor of a church or a shepherd of a small flock in your home?

Do you have passion, compassion, and a deep love for every Christian?

List what you believe are the five top qualifications for this office:

Time to Grow

Do you feel that you've supported your current pastor and leaders?

If not, why?

If so, why?

If there are any walls between you and your pastor, or any of the congregants in your church, think of ways to bring them down in a loving, godly way.

25

Other Gifts

"And since we have gifts that differ, according to the grace given to us, let each exercise them accordingly."
Romans 12:6a

Not all of the gifts are listed together in one place in the Bible, but filter throughout its pages. Gifts that suit us well, that we can learn to utilize within the guidelines of the Holy Spirit. He will direct us in all things and sharpen the gifts within us. Perhaps some of us have not recognized these following gifts. Here are some of them:

• Intercessory Prayer: To pray without ceasing until enemy strongholds are broken and breakthroughs come to light.

> *"For this reason, also, since the day we heard of it, we have not ceased to pray for you and to ask that you may be filled with the knowledge of His will in all spiritual wisdom and understanding."*
> Colossians 1:9

- Celibacy: The spiritual ability to enjoy being single and also to maintain sexual self-control.

   "Yet I wish that all men were even as I myself am. However, each man has his own gift from God, one in this manner, and another in that. But I say to the unmarried and to widows that it is good for them if they remain even as I."
   1 Corinthians 7:7–8

- Voluntary poverty: To live a unique lifestyle of relative poverty by renouncing material comfort and gain.

   "Keep deception and lies far from me, give me neither poverty nor riches."
   Proverbs 30:8

- Martyrdom: Willing to endure persecution, suffering, and even death for one's faith in the anointing of the Holy Spirit.

   "And if I give all my possessions to feed the poor, and if I deliver my body to be burned..."
   1 Corinthians 13:3a

- Hospitality: The ability and desire to offer your home and meals to those in want, or to strangers. The gift that keeps giving and never tires of doing so. One might have the gift of giving along with the gift of hospitality.

   "Be hospitable to one another without complaint."
   1 Peter 4:9

OTHER GIFTS

- Missionary work: The desire to travel to far-off countries to bring the good news of the gospel, supplies, and helps.

> *"Go into all the world and preach the gospel to all creation."*
> Acts 16:15

- Exorcism: The ability with the spiritual gift of discernment to cast out demons from people.

> *"In my name, they will cast out demons."*
> Mark 16:17a

All gifts are useful and profitable while used in the admonition of the Holy Spirit, along with a servant's heart.

Time to Weigh In

Take a few moments to reflect back to your childhood, while asking yourself what you were always good at. Pray that God will show you the gifts He's already given you.

Were you aware of certain skills and tasks you performed in high school and college?

Did those skills remain and grow with you into adulthood?

What skills heightened once you were born again?

Make a list of all jobs you've had up until now:

Write down the very special ones like parenting and teaching. Taking care of an elder or a small child:

How do you imagine helping others?

Have you had a goal, dream, or vision in your past that clearly showed you how to serve God and the Body of Christ that hasn't manifested yet?

Time to Grow

Have you ever learned about the gifts before?

If so, have you received any gifting?

List your one or more gifts:

How do you believe that your gifts can be enhanced?

Do you use them as the Holy Spirit guides you?

Have you shared your gifts with your pastor or other leaders in your church?

If so, did they respond with encouragement?

If you have not received any gifts at this time, which of the service gifts interest you?

Let's journey on to the next chapter on how to receive your gifts, and to use them in the anointing of the Holy Spirit.

26

How to Receive Your Gifts

"Pursue love, yet desire earnestly spiritual gifts, but especially that you may prophesy."
                                                1 Corinthians 14:1

Gifts from God are instruments to enable normal people like you and me to help other normal people. To minister to them in the anointing of the wondrous Holy Spirit. The gifts are great assets for us to cherish and to share with others.

I'm grateful for the gifts I've received from the Holy Spirit. It's been a spiritual experience that has brought both growth and rewards. You might also share this joy, to move in the Spirit with your gifts. If you've not yet done so and would like to discover them—or find any that haven't been released in your life yet—I exhort you to start with prayer.

Ask the Holy Spirit to guide you in your discovery. (Remember that God loves to shower His children with many gifts.) Then answer the following questions, followed by a thought-provoking questions for you. You can write in your answers below each one:

1. Have I had a desire to receive the gifts of the Holy Spirit while reading this book?

• If so, which of the supernatural and service gifts did you get motivated by while studying them?

2. Will I be content with one gift, or many?

• Having several gifts requires obedience and self-sacrifice. How much time do you devote to studying the Word, and in prayer?

3. Do I recognize that my given gifts will manifest by the Holy Spirit, and not by me?

• Are you good at yielding to listen? The Holy Spirit will guide you and give you what to say. Are you able to put yourself aside and let Him glow?

4. Am I willing to further the kingdom of God while sacrificing worldly things?

- Can you identify the worldly things you would be giving up? If you can, then write them down and then cross them out as an act of faith.

5. Is my walk with God consistent with the gospel so that He'll make me a vessel for His glory?

- How long have you been a Christian? Are you still drinking spiritual milk, or have you moved onto meat? Sometimes a believer will recognize and use their gifts directly upon being born again. Others might take longer to begin. It's when we fully understand the importance of serving others that we start to see more clearly in the Spirit.

6. Am I able to distinguish the difference between spiritual and natural talents?

- We all have natural talents. Write down a list of those that you believe you have, then write down the spiritual and service gifts you believe you might have. As you do, remember that God is able to gift you now with new gifts that you may not have had yet.

7. Am I truly willing to give my time to God and His purposes? To change my lifestyle and priorities to serve Him? Will I be available to answer His call?

- It takes time and devotion to learn how to hear and obey the voice of God and His instructions. Is this a priority in your life? If it hasn't been, do you want it to be now?

8. Will I give God all the glory, and none to myself?

- It is absolutely necessary to give God all the glory, as He works through you to touch others' lives. At times we might be tempted to take a little of the glory for ourselves. How would you control this temptation if it arises?

HOW TO RECEIVE YOUR GIFTS

Thank you for taking the time to answer these important questions. Once you've finished and are ready to move forward, please start with this prayer:

Heavenly Father, thank You for saving me and giving me Your Holy Spirit. I'm asking You to baptize me afresh in Your power and anointing. I have studied about the gifts and am ready to receive everything You have for me. To bless the brethren and to do good works for You.

I ask that You would show me my gifts, and how to use them with confidence and great joy. That You would make me aware of the needs of the people around me. Open my eyes that I may see in the spiritual realm.

Help me to put my own ambitions aside and to follow Your example to me by Your Word and the prompting of the Holy Spirit. And above all things, to give You all the glory.

In Jesus' name, amen.

Time to Weigh In

How do you feel now after praying about receiving gifts from the Holy Spirit? (Be candid and specific.)

Time to Grow

It's time to go further into developing a sense of how to use your gifting. In this next chapter, we will discuss how to stay in the anointing of the Holy Spirit as we do. Are you ready?

27

How to Use Your Gifts

"Therefore, holy brethren, partakers of a heavenly calling, consider Jesus, the Apostle and High Priest of our confession. He was faithful to Him who appointed Him."
Hebrews 1:1–2a

The first thing to do as we start to put our gifts to good use is to ask the Holy Spirit to anoint us with truth. To let Him know that we are servants who earnestly desire to bring forth His glory through the gifts He's blessed us with. If we yield to Him to work through us, He surely will.

Secondly, to acknowledge God's faithfulness in our lives. As we lay aside our own thoughts and ambitions, God will minister through us to others for His own purposes. And even if a word comes to us that we don't quite understand yet, we can choose to trust that *He* does. A word or direction from God that can sound insignificant to us could have a great impact on someone else.

Once I received a word from God to share with a person that I hesitated to say. After stalling, it seemed that my chest started to burn that good-ole Holy Spirit conviction burn. So I spoke the seemingly silly word, which turned out to be true and very beneficial to the person's health.

The biggest help in successfully using our gifts is to trust that God will never fail us. Once we've used our gift, we'll be more confident the next time the opportunity arises.

We must keep ourselves grounded in biblical truths and guidelines for the gifts. One way is to sit under a good Bible teacher for a season, and another is to have fellowship with other Christians who usually flow in the gifts of the Holy Spirit. We can participate in Bible studies where this normally occurs.

Remember that ability and accuracy comes when we surrender to the flow of the Holy Spirit. A small group is a good place to start practicing our gifting. Others that have gifts might help us along as we step out for the first time.

As we do step out in faith, God will affirm and establish us in our ministries. We'll receive positive feedback from those we've ministered to and have had fellowship with. Let's be open to their praise as well as their constructive comments. This will refine our use of the Spirit's gifts.

I'd like to share a word of warning with you. There are some who seem to have gifts, but aren't using them properly. They might not be hearing from God—but from the enemy—or thoughts of their own. Ask God to give you discernment concerning this when you go to a group that moves in any kind of spiritual gifts.

As we utilize our gifts over a period of time, they will prove to be pure. From God, and without human input. What we don't want to do is to conjure up supernatural manifestations from God. To try and make something happen in our flesh will prove to be wrong, and possibly disastrous.

If we step out in the flesh and try to muster up gifts from the Holy Spirit, we might appear to look like a magician who's act went terribly wrong. This could bring humiliation for us and a disappointment for others.

Our gifts are designed for the edification, guidance, and benefit of others. We should only benefit secondly. And remember that gifts can be misused if they are in the power of the flesh, not the Spirit. We need to use our gifts in love, and in the proper order, or they will be of no value.

We, as believers, have certain duties in the same areas of gifting. For instance, we have roles in helps, mercy, giving, intercession, hospitality, and much more—even if we don't have the "gift" of those services.

A good thing to ask ourselves is how our spiritual gifts relate both to unity and diversity within our Church. We can learn to discern between the fruit of the Spirit, spiritual gifts, and natural talents. Sounds overwhelming, but in time, our Teacher, the Holy Spirit, schools us in these graces.

Glance with me at this list of some things to watch for and to remember when using your prophetic gifts:

1. Are the congregants open to the movement of the Holy Spirit? If they seemingly aren't, then schedule a meeting with your leaders and discuss how you can gracefully implement your gifts into the church.

2. When you are receiving a gift such as a word of knowledge, wisdom, or prophecy, hold on to it for a while. Ask God if He's showing you this so that you'll know how to pray for someone, or if He wants for you to deliver that word to them personally. As you wait upon the Lord, the Holy Spirit will show you.

3. There is an appropriate time to use your gifts. Make sure that you're being led by the Spirit, and not your flesh. For example, if you were to receive an utterance from God during the church announcements, it might be a good idea for you to hang on to it until a time of worship or prayer.

4. Consider if you're wanting to draw attention to yourself or to God each time you believe that you have a prompting from the Holy Spirit. It's important to speak out under the influence of God, not of your own.

5. If you get a word that you're not sure of, you can share it with another believer who moves in the gifts. They hopefully can confirm with you whether to speak that word then, or to hold on to it for a time.

6. Make sure that you pray before each meeting that God will use you. Die to self and become alive in Christ.

7. As for other gifts, always pray first for the anointing of God. Before you take on an office of service, or before you lay hands on another for healing. In all things, give thanks to God.

8. As for the service gifts, ask yourself if you are being led by the Lord, or if you're striving. Regardless, hardly any service gift is turned away. But we need to make sure that our hearts are right before we commit to a particular service.

Time to Weigh In

How do you feel after reading the eight suggestions in this chapter?

Are you ready to begin using the gifts from the Holy Spirit now?

Time to Grow

In what areas would you like to change your heart and attitude in regards to the gifts that have already been given to you?

Are you hungry for more gifts?

If so, ask and you'll receive according to God's will and purposes in your life.

28

Holy Spirit Come

"And it shall be in the last days," God says, 'That I will pour forth of my Spirit on all mankind; and your sons and your daughters shall prophesy, and your young men shall see visions, and your old men shall dream dreams; Even on my bond slaves, both men and women, I will in those days pour of My Spirit and they shall prophesy. And I will grant wonders in the sky above and signs on the earth below, blood, and fire, and vapor of smoke. The sun will be turned into darkness and the moon into blood, before the great and glorious day of the Lord shall come. And it shall be that everyone who calls on the name of the Lord will be saved.'"

Acts 2:17–21

Precious brothers and sisters, we are in the end of days. Let's prepare and sharpen our spiritual swords and receive our gifts for the battles ahead. To bring forth victory in the name of our Lord, and in the power of the Holy Spirit. To do the work that God's asked us to do in the name of His Son, Jesus. To be filled with the glorious Holy Spirit every waking day and fulfill His purposes in our lives as we work toward the day of His return.

This is our invitation to join in on the most unimaginably awesome event of history. And that's why we were born now. Every one of us have been personally appointed by God to be used by Him and His Holy Spirit. Each of us suited in God's armor, and equipped with priceless gifts. God makes no mistakes. He knew before we were born that we'd obey Him. And now, more than any other time, He will use us.

God is spirit and cannot be seen. He appeared in a bush as fire, so that Moses could better see and sense His presence. Same for today. We have the Holy Spirit living in us—therefore others should see God in us through our behavior, obedience, and the manifestations of the Holy Spirit through us in our gifts. God dwells within us to display His radiance, glory, and presence. Therefore, as the fire in the bush shone in the dark to Moses, it will also bring forth God's light to others through us.

When we open up for God to use us, we need not worry of what we'll say. The Spirit will give us words when we need them. He has fully equipped us to prevail in the times of trouble.

WE WILL BE VICTORIOUS IN HIS NAME!

We are living in a time of spiritual warfare. Good against evil. Light against darkness. Truth against falsehood. We must fight the good fight in the power of the Holy Spirit.

> *"For though we walk in the flesh, we do not war according to the flesh, for the weapons of our warfare are not of the flesh, but divinely powerful for the destruction of fortresses."*
> 2 Corinthians 10:3–4

We already know what we're up against. Let's be aware of what the Scriptures say:

> *"For our struggle is not against flesh and blood, but against the rulers, against the powers, against the world forces of this darkness, against the spiritual forces of wickedness in the heavenly places."*
> Ephesians 6:12

A good thing to remember is that we do not fight against people but spirits. Cultists, false religionists, atheists, agnostics, and pseudo-Christians are at times used by demons influencing them. But greater is Jesus in us, regardless of the outcome. We can trust that He has the perfect plan all the way around. And our reward: eternal life with Him.

Will the Holy Spirit protect us during this time of warfare?

This is a good question, but a hard one to answer. The Holy Spirit has worked through wonderful men and women of God who have been killed for their faith. Jesus warned us with His own words of the persecution to come:

> *"Then they will deliver you to tribulation, and will kill you, and you will be hated by all nations because of My name. At that time many will fall away and will betray one another and hate one another. Many false prophets will arise and will mislead many. Because lawlessness is increased, most people's love will grow cold. But the one who endures to the end, he will be saved."*
> Matthew 24:9–13

This Scripture warns us of things to come. It's dreadfully sad that some will indeed be killed for the Lord's sake. But we have another home to go to that will not perish:

"For to me, to live is Christ and to die is gain."
Philippians 1:21

Paul knew danger awaited him. To be with Christ would be the most wonderful thing of two worlds. But he understood the depth of importance to stay on. More souls had to be saved.

And this is the attitude and belief that we also need to have. The desire to be with Christ, and yet the zeal to stay and help do the work God has given us for this tumultuous time.

We can continue to do the work that the Lord has set before us, while inviting the help of the Holy Spirit. He works through those who are willing to perform the supernatural. We are only here for a short time. So, let's make that time worthy of our wonderful God who awaits us in heaven!

AFTERWORD

If you have read this book and desire to get to know your God, I lovingly invite you to join His family by saying this prayer:

Heavenly Father,
 I believe that Jesus Christ is Your Son and that He died for my sins. I believe that He rose from the dead three days later, and resides with You in your throne room.
 I ask You to forgive my sins and make me whole—a new creature in Christ. I ask for the Holy Spirit to live in me, so that I may be gifted and carry on the work that You started here. Thank You for redeeming me through the shed blood of Your Son.
 In Jesus' name, amen.

After you've said this prayer, I would like to encourage you to find a good church and Bible study to attend. Develop fellowship with other believers. You could start reading the Word, beginning with *The Gospel According to John.*

Find a trustworthy and wise prayer partner and stay accountable to them. Pray without ceasing and love others as you love yourself. May God bless your journey!

And, to the believer: I hope you enjoyed hearing how God has so generously worked in my life. If you haven't already experienced the Holy Spirit in *your* life, I pray that you will be open to all that

He has for you—that you will see His amazing, supernatural power and grace first-hand. Once you are open to the gifts, you can yield and receive.

I challenge you to brave the unknown—to let go of the old, and enter into the new world of His glory. Ask the Holy Spirit to gift you and teach you about those graces that He has, especially for you. Venture out anew, into the depths of His living water—where the fish are plentiful and the blessings are without end.

Dear Reader,

Thanks so very much for the time you've taken to read my book. I hope it was an inspiration to you.

Would you consider sharing something about your reading experience? If so, please visit this book's Amazon page online and post your review there.

Readers all over the world benefit from comments such as yours, and I'll truly appreciate your feedback.

Blessings,
Connie

ABOUT THE AUTHOR

CONNIE ENGEL moved from Claremont, California to Los Angeles to pursue a career as a television commercial actress and model. While spending many years jet-setting around the world, she felt a void. That void—the absence of God in her life. In 1980, she dedicated herself to the Lord, and her life profoundly changed. In 1981, she married Executive Producer, Peter Engel.

Soon after, she had her two sons, Joshua and Stephen. Motherhood has been her happiest, most fulfilling years. Connie and her husband prayed for a television show they could make for children. God blessed them with *Saved by the Bell* and other shows as well, including: *Hang Time, USA High, City Guys, Malibu, CA, One World, California Dreams, Saved by the Bell—the New Class, Saved by the Bell—the College Years,* and two television movies: *Saved by the Bell—Hawaiian Style,* and *Saved by the Bell—Wedding in Las Vegas.*

Connie also loved to paint and developed a career which landed her into several national galleries and a contract with Winn Devon Publishers. She has been teaching the Bible to women for thirty years, as of this publication.

Would you like to receive a biblical encouragement via email each day? If so, Connie invites you to sign up at this address:

http://www.conniesencouragement.blogspot.com

Her love for God, family, and others has inspired her to share the supernatural events that God has created in her life. Connie's greatest desire is to *finish well*.

BOOKS BY CONNIE BRYSON ENGEL

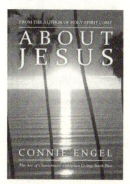

Book Two of The Art of
Charismatic Christian Living Series

https://www.amazon.com/dp/B07NZ8ZLN7

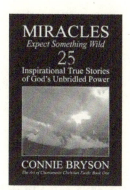

Book One of The Art of
Charismatic Christian Faith Series

http://www.amazon.com/MIRACLES-Something-Inspirational-Unbridled-Charismatic-ebook/dp/B00M3FV0CM

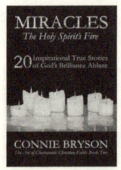

Book Two of the Art of
Charismatic Christian Faith Series

http://www.amazon.com/MIRACLES-Inspirational-Brilliance-Charismatic-Christian-ebook/dp/B00OVLLG02

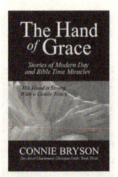

Book Three of the Art of
Charismatic Christian Faith Series

http://www.amazon.com/dp/B00VVWMUEK

Book One of the Art of God's Creation Series

http://www.amazon.com/POEMS-SUMMER-Delightful-Descriptions-Creation-ebook/dp/B00W4ZO31Q

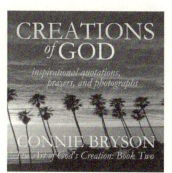

Book Two of the Art of God's Creation Series

http://www.amazon.com/dp/B010CDLTL8

Made in the USA
Las Vegas, NV
09 March 2024